W9-CJG-164

HOLIDAY Collectibles

Vintage Flea Market Treasures

Lissa Bryan-Smith and Richard Smith

© 1998 by

Lissa Bryan-Smith and Richard Smith

All rights reserved. No portion of this publication may be reproduced or transmitted in any form or by any means, electronic or mechanical, including photocopy, recording, or any information storage and retrieval system, without permission in writing from the publisher, except by a reviewer who may quote brief passages in a critical article or review to be printed in a magazine or newspaper, or electronically transmitted on radio or television.

Published by

**krause
publications**

700 E. State Street • Iola, WI 54990-0001
Telephone: 715/445-2214

Please call or write for our free catalog.
Our toll-free number to place an order or obtain a free catalog is 800-258-0929
or please use our regular business telephone 715-445-2214 for editorial comment and further information.
Photographs by Ken Roszel of Roszel Photography.

ISBN: 0-87069-769-2
Library of Congress: 98-84092
Printed in the United States of America

TABLE OF CONTENTS

FOREWORD

Treasure hunting is as old as man. The lure of finding a sunken ship, a buried pirate's chest, or stagecoach robber's hidden gold can fill a lifetime. Join this innate desire with an interest in a particular category of objects, and you have a collector. When the category of interest is the holidays that highlight our year, a passion is born.

Like following a pirate's secret map, every flea market booth, yard sale, or antique shop just might have a new item to decorate with. This search can add enrichment to your days, and every trip to a new area of the country or the world opens new swap meets and flea markets just as X marks the spot on the pirate's map.

Collecting adds many hours of enjoyment to your life. Reading the books on holidays and holiday antiques builds a new appreciation for our celebrations and customs. This adds new respect for those people and cultures that have come before us. Researching how these decorations were made also contributes to their fascination and provides many insights into times past. We wish you many hours of pleasure in hunting and decorating with your antique holiday finds. We also hope this book will help you in your search.

INTRODUCTION

The materials used in antique decorations may not be familiar in this age of plastic and acrylic. We have used a variety of terms in describing the ornaments.

Glass is a commonly used material, especially for Christmas decorations. When the glass itself is colored, it is usually referred to as art glass. Blown glass ornaments are usually clear glass that is used either alone, silvered on the inside and/or colored on the outside. After a glass ornament was shaped, it was silvered by pouring a mixture of nitrate, quick lime and milk sugar inside. After shaking to evenly coat the inside, the excess is poured out and the ornament is allowed to dry. This gives a mirror-like appearance to the ornament. Color was added to either a silvered or unsilvered ornament by dipping the outside in translucent lacquer paint. After this had dried, details in various colors and materials were added by brush.

A number of different materials were used to form objects and figures for all our holidays. Papier-mâché may be familiar as the material we used as children. This was bits or strips of paper softened in glue. Commercially, the paper is reduced to a slurry and combined with glue. The figure is usually formed in a mold, that when dried forms a detailed and durable object.

Variations on this technique were developed at various times and used over a long period. Molded cardboard is the forming of three-dimensional figures with heat and moisture from whole pieces of cardboard. We use the term "egg crate" for a cardboard-like material identical to the material used for the boxes used to hold eggs. This material has a distinctive pattern on the surface and was used for Santa Claus, turkeys and pumpkins among others. A common material for all the holidays is a composition often referred to as "compo." It is a material used for molded figures and is a combination of sawdust, glue, clay and flour.

Celluloid was the first "plastic." Invented in England, celluloid was first used for manufacturing in 1869 in New Jersey. Toys and decorations were made of this product in great numbers until the need for the raw materials during World War II decreased the use. It was last produced in the early 1950s. Celluloid is made from cotton dissolved by nitric acid.

This "pulp" is mixed with camphor gum and formed into flat sheets. Celluloid is easily molded with the application of heat.

Early plastic is a hard, shiny and brittle substance. It has an almost glass-like appearance. In this book, we refer to this as "hard plastic" as opposed to the more currently produced plastic which is softer and more flexible. When collecting a major factor in price and desirability is the condition of the item. While some wear often confirms an object's age, obvious damage frequently makes an item worthless. Prices in this book are for items without significant damage.

For the collector interested in only original holiday decorations, reproductions are a common problem. Almost everything in this collecting field is being reproduced and often presented by the unscrupulous or uninformed as "old." One way to guard against this is to be familiar with what is being manufactured today. One of the best sources for today's output is the catalog. These companies present the current output of Germany and other countries. Another source for "reproductions" is the current "craft" craze. Many reputable crafters produce models of yesterday's decorations that they proudly sign. An unfortunate practice is for someone to purchase the crafted item, remove the part with the signature, add some "age" and retail the object as antique.

The prices in this book are based on a year-round sample of the market. We traveled to all areas of the country and visited flea markets, swap meets, antique shows and antique shops. We subscribe to mail-order lists and of course attend auctions and tag sales. We have tried to list the average price. It is not unusual for holiday items to be both overpriced and underpriced by dealers. Of course everybody enjoys finding the "steal" and everyone moans when an item is overpriced. Everyone must make a decision at some point to pay more than what is probably reasonable for an unusual item to add to the collection.

One final note. Each collector sets his or her own age limits. Whether you concentrate on the Victorian era or the "Fifties," the idea is to enjoy holiday collecting from the hunt to arranging the display.

CHAPTER 1

VALENTINE'S DAY

A Roman holiday and a Christian saint are the legendary foundations for our Valentine's Day holiday. Lupercalia, the festival for the Roman god Faunus, was celebrated on February 15th. Faunus, whose temple was a cave on Palatine Hill in Rome, is the god of animal life, husbandry, herding and guardian of the secrets of nature. His cave, according to legend, was the site where Romulus and Remus were raised by a wolf.

In the third century, Claudius II imprisoned a Christian priest named Valentinus for aiding fellow Christians during persecution. While confined, it is said he befriended the blind daughter of his jailer and restored her sight. His farewell note to the girl was signed "from your Valentinus," paving the way for millions of future cards signed "from your valentine."

The feast of Lupercalia was transported to Britain with the Roman conquest. There it evolved into a spring festival where boys and girls drew names for their partners during the celebration. Many times this pairing resulted in marriage. As Christianity competed with paganism the Christian priests sought opportunities to allow the people to still celebrate the popular festivals. They wisely associated the pagan festivals with Christian saints. In this instance, Lupercalia, the spring festival and the martyrdom of Saint Valentinus became Saint Valentine's Day.

The tradition of exchanging names developed into the custom of also exchanging gifts and mottoes. As so often happens, the gifts became more and more expensive. As a result, the custom gradually changed to sending mottoes or cards in lieu of a gift.

As the Romans brought the holiday to England, the English brought St. Valentine's Day to America. But the holiday did not gain widespread popularity until the Eighteenth century. Early cards or mottoes were handmade. Some were simple but many were very detailed. The sentiments included were either original or they could be copied from books known as "valentine writers" published specifically for the purpose of penning and answering valentines. The mottoes were rarely sent by post, due to the cost. They were usually hand-delivered and left at the maiden's door.

Several themes have remained constant in valentine sentiments. Cupid, of mythological fame, was popular because of the legend that his arrow could sway the heart that it pierced. Birds are also pictured on valentines. It was believed in the 1400s that birds mated on February 14th, so they became entwined in the legend. Of course almost every valentine features a flower. The two most popular are the rose and the violet. Both, in the language of flowers have always been associated with romance.

Although the early valentines were handmade, certain styles were popular. Puzzles, cutouts and pinpricks were common in the 1700s. The detailed pinprick and cutouts were the models for the "doilies" sold today for valentine decorations. Clever businessmen noted the potential market for manufactured greetings. By the 19th century, the valentine card was a commercial success. Printed and lithographed cards started to replace handmade valentines.

The valentine found a champion in the United States. Her name was Esther Howland. She was unusual for her time, because in 1847, she graduated from Mount Holyoke College. Her father owned a stationery and bookseller business in Worcester, Massachusetts. He also was unusual for his era because he encouraged her fascination with valentines. She designed several the year she graduated from col-

Heart-shaped box, cardboard, red and white with red satin ribbon, mkd. "Daggett Lion Crest Brand," 10" h $18

Heart-shaped boxes, L-R, L: cardboard, "To My Valentine," mkd. "Germany," 5" h $30; R: cardboard, satin covered, hinged top, scrap angel on front, mkd. "Germany," 2-1/2" h $25

the popularity of her valentines spread until her orders were going out all over the country. She eventually built her own business – The New England Valentine Company. Her cards are identified by a small "H" stamped in red in a corner of the back page, a white heart glued on the back page with the stamped "H," or a glued on label with "H." Later cards have the mark of her company; "N.E.V.Co." embossed on the back of the card.

The town of Worcester was truly the valentine capital of the United States during the 19th century. George Whitney jumped on the valentine bandwagon created by Esther Howland. By the 1860s, he was producing valentines quite similar to Howland. He identified his early cards with a stamped "W" on the back. He aggressively bought out his competitors and eventually purchased Esther Howland's company. The Whitney Company was the leader in valentine manufacturing in the U.S. for decades.

Collectors today often collect valentines by category. Some only collect mechanical valentines (cards with moving parts), transportation cards (trains, ships, airships, automobile), animals cards or dimensional valentines. The price of a valentine often reflects the tastes of its collectors.

lege and they were shown with other samples to her father's potential customers throughout New England. She received orders for thousands. She and several of her friends completed the first orders and

Candy Containers

Heart-shaped box, cardboard, red and white, "To My Valentine," troubadour playing mandolin to a lady in front of castle pictured on cover, USA, 10" h . . $20

Magazines

Child Life, February 1943, valentine card on cover $10
Home Arts, February 1930, Little girl stitching a valentine handkerchief on cover. $8
Ladies' Home Journal, February 1936, woman in red dress on cover $12
The Ladies' World, February 1900, woman surrounded by cupids with a net. $15

Paper

Calling Cards

Rectangular, cupid in wisteria arbor by lake, "Happy Valentine's Greetings," mkd. "Gibson Lines, Cincinnati and New York," 2-1/4" h $4

Greeting Cards

Dimensional

Foldout, 3-dimensional with honeycomb inserts, birdhouse on tall pole surrounded by cupids, flowers and doves, 13" h $75
Fold-out, boy and girl surrounded by snowdrops, forget-me-nots and roses, honeycomb, "To My Valentine," mkd. "Printed in Germany," 5-1/2" h . $12

Foldout, boy playing mandolin to girl, lithographed with honeycomb, "To My Valentine," 6" h $7
Fold-out, cupids and white doves with blue and pink tissue paper flowers, "With Best Wishes," 5-1/2" h $8
Fold-out, girl in wreath of roses, 6" h $4

Flat

Easel back, embossed heart with three children carrying gifts in snow, "St. Valentine's Greeting,"mkd. with an "E" in a circle, 6-1/2" h $6
Embossed, pastel colors, three sections, yellow rose, harp with flowers, "My Heart is Thine," hanging, 19" l. $45

Heart-shaped boxes, L-R, L: cardboard, red and white, 4"h $10; R: cardboard, red, white and silver, "Valentine Greetings," 4" h $12

Embossed, heart-shaped, a baby in roses surrounded by violets, "To One I Love," 5" h $6

Rectangular, girl and cat at a tea party, "As soon as Kitty has had her Tea," mkd. "Printed in Bavaria, Ernest Nister, London #830," 3" h $5

Folded

Heart-shaped, girl in circle surrounded by hearts, mkd. "Whitney Made, Worcester, Mass," 4" h . $3

Rectangular, boy and a girl picking flowers, "For My Valentine," 3-3/4" h $3

Rectangular, girl holding key by locked door, "Help! Please! Oh Please Open This! And Be My Valentine," mkd. "E Series No. 143 Valentine, 5 Designs," 5" h $8

Rectangular, mother holding little girl, "From a Faithful Friend With Love Sincere," 5" h $15

Honeycomb

Ballerina, with honeycomb tutu, "To My Valentine," mkd. "Printed in Germany," 1930, 7" h $6

Boy artist painting a portrait of a girl, "I'd Love To Paint You My Valentine," honeycomb at base, mkd. "Made in USA," 6" h $5

Cupid with mail, "To My Sweetheart," honeycomb at base and top, mkd. "Made in USA," 5" h $7

Mechanical

Easel back, ferris wheel with children, brightly lithographed, ferris wheel turns when a string is pulled, "Tell You Who Is My Valentine," mkd. "Made in Germany," 9" h. $20

Easel back, girl and boy in doorway, lithographed, a tug on the girl opens the door to show the boy, mkd. "Printed in Germany," 6" h $15

Postcards

"A Valentine Thought," cupid sitting on heart. . . . $2

Heart-shaped box, cardboard, red, white and gold, "Valentine Greetings," 10" h $20

"A Wish That Comes From The Heart," a wishbone over a heart, 1911 . . . . $3

"I'll Arrest Any Fellow Who Tries To Steal My Girl," boy dressed as policeman, mkd. "Made in USA," 1916. . . . . $3

"I'm Falling For You Kid," boy and girl roller skating, mkd. "Made in USA," 1916 . . . . $3

"Somebody Charming; I Wonder Who? A Little Bird Whispers To Me "Tis You," boy holding basket of hearts, mkd. "Whitney Made, Worcester, Mass, Made in USA," 1923 . . . . $4

"To My Sweet Valentine," cupid delivering flowers to lady in window, sepia tones. $3

"To My Valentine," cupid shooting arrow, mkd. "Made in USA," 1924. . . . . $2

"To My Valentine With Love," girl in heart surrounded by pink flowers, B.B. London, Series No.1507, printed in Germany $3

Nut/candy cups, red crepe paper with red and green crepe paper rose, 4" h $4 ea.

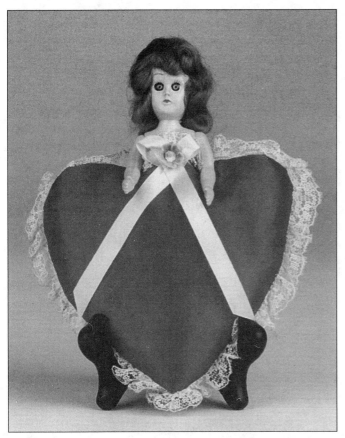

Doll, red satin pillow, hard plastic torso and head with sleepy eyes, 1950s, 7" h $15

Hard plastic, red and white, USA, 4" h $15

Ladies' Home Journal, *February 1937 $15*

Dimensional, gondola, lithographed, embossed, red honeycomb inserts, 10-1/2" l $75

Dimensional, lithographed, embossed, mkd. "Germany," 9" h $30

Flats, L-R, L: dog, easel back, mkd. "Printed in Germany," 5-1/2" h $10; R: parrot, easel back, mkd "Made in Germany," 4-1/2" h $5

Flats, L-R, L: easel back, 7-1/2" h $12; R: easel back, embossed, 7" h $5

Flat, automobile, embossed, 15" l $90

Folded and lithographed, Top: mkd. "Whitney Made, Worcester, Mass," 3-1/2" h $3; L: 4" h $4; R: 1933, 3-1/2" h $3

Booklet with string binding, embossed cover, inside pages have lithographed pictures and verse, 4" h $10

Honeycomb, foldout, mkd. "Made in USA," 8" h $12

Honeycomb, fold-out, 9" h $25

Mechanical, eyes of the stork move as the baby rocks, easel back, mkd. "Made in Germany," 8" h $18

Postcards, signed, "Ellen H. Clapsaddle," L-R, L: 1922, mkd. "Printed in Germany"; R: mkd. "Made in USA," $10 ea.

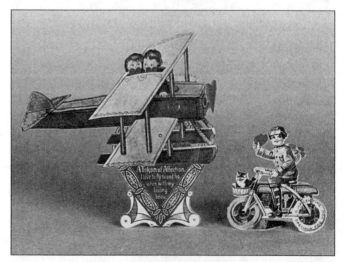

Mechanical, L-R, L: airplane moves back and forth, easel back, 7" h $30; R: motorcycle, wheel turn and arms wave, mkd. "Printed in Germany," 4" h $15

Flat, L-R, L: boy on phone, mkd. "Germany," easel back, 4-1/2" h $5; Middle: Mechanical, cat, when ribbon on neck is pulled face changes, mkd. "Made in Germany," 5" h $10; R: Cat, listening to radio, mkd. "Germany," 3-1/2" h $7

Folded, paper lace, lithographed and embossed, L-R, L: 6" h $15; Middle: 8-1/2" h $20; R: 6" h $15

CHAPTER 2

ST. PATRICK'S DAY

A highly popular secular holiday in the United States and a quiet religious observance in Ireland characterize the St. Patrick's holiday. On March 17th, in the United States, everyone pretends to be Irish. St. Patrick's life is as much legend as fact. Born in Roman England, he was captured as a boy and taken into slavery in Ireland. There, while herding sheep, he experienced a vision telling him to escape by sea. Finding a ship waiting, he sailed for three days and landed in either Brittany or Britain. He and his crew were saved from starvation by a herd of wild pigs, which arrived in answer to Patrick's prayer. He continued to have dreams and visions which caused Patrick to study in various centers of Christian learning. He eventually became a priest.

Legend tells that in a dream Patrick saw a man approaching with a letter. The letter was from the people of Ireland and read, "We beseech thee, holy youth, to come and walk once more amongst us." Patrick returned to Ireland, and while performing many miracles, established and organized Christianity.

Ireland of this time was led by the Druids. Patrick was forced to compete with them to establish his church. One story is that Father Patrick used the native plant, the shamrock, with its distinctive three-part leaf to illustrate the Christian concept of the Holy Trinity. From this parable, the shamrock became the symbol of the nation of Ireland.

The most famous miracle St. Patrick performed in Ireland was the ridding of the land of snakes and vermin. It is said he drove them out with the sound of a drum. The story goes that early in this miracle, the drum broke to the great relief of the snakes. However, an angel appeared and healed the tear in the drum.

As a result of all St. Patrick's efforts, Ireland became a Christian nation, and they honor their patron saint to this day. March 17th is celebrated as St. Patrick's Day. It is not known whether this date was of his birth or his death.

St. Patrick's Day in America is a true festival marked by parties, family gatherings and parades. The holiday was first celebrated in 1737 in Boston. On March 17, 1776, the British evacuated Boston. The patriot forces consequently used the password "Boston" and the countersign "St. Patrick." The Irish were truly entrenched in the history of the New World.

The potato famine in Ireland in the mid-1800s forced a huge percentage of the population to im-

migrate to other countries. Large numbers of Irish poured into the United States over the next several decades. They brought with them their traditions and religious beliefs. Irish immigrants were not embraced by the United States and they settled close together to try to alleviate their homesickness for Ireland and their families. St. Patrick's Day took on an even greater importance to the Irish Americans, because it was another way to celebrate their heritage. The festivities spread and gained in popularity with all Americans.

Manufacturers of holiday goods recognized another opportunity and started producing decorations and greetings for St. Patrick's Day. Many of the symbols and decorations they chose to represent the holiday were derived from Ireland and the legends of St. Patrick. Other symbols were borrowed from the stereotypes created by threatened citizens of the countries that experienced the Irish influx.

Harp, diecut, embossed, 3" h $12

The symbols cover a wide spectrum. The pig commemorates the saint's rescue from starvation. The association of the color green is from the verdant countryside of Ireland. The shamrock, as previously described, has become the universal symbol of the Irish. Many decorations, greeting cards, postcards and banners over the years have carried the phrase, "Erin Go Bragh" which means "Ireland Forever" in the Gaelic language. This was especially meaningful to the Irish Americans that felt very strongly about Irish independence from Britain. The potato was the main food and economic resource for people in Ireland in the early 1800s and the Irish were often referred to as "potato eaters." The famine cemented the association of the Irish and the potato. Consequently, many decorations feature a potato. A harp, beer and the generic name of "Paddy" for anyone Irish all frequently appear as themes in the holiday decorations.

Candy Container

Bust of Irishman, top hat and clay pipe, papier-mâché, opening in bottom, Germany, 4-1/2" h $110

Head of a pig mounted on the end of a noisemaker, wearing green and gold top hat, pig is papier-mâché, hat and noisemaker are cardboard, hat opens to hold candy, 8" l $130

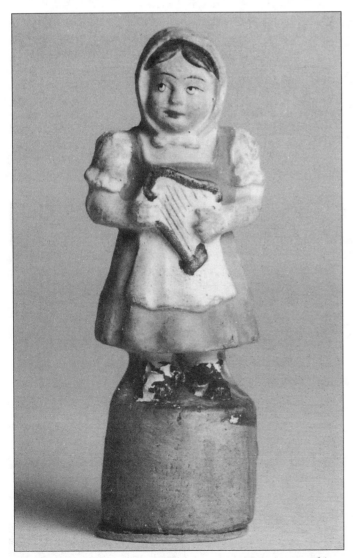

Girl holding harp, candy container, composition, green, white, black and brown, opening in base, mkd. "Germany," 4-1/2" h $90

Irish boy, standing on top of candy box, boy is papier-mâché, box is cardboard, mkd. "Box Made In Germany," 4-1/2" h $150

Irish boy and girl, standing on top of candy box, figures are papier-mâché, box is cardboard, Germany, 4" h $185

Irish Whiskey bottle, cardboard and lithographed paper, Germany, 5-1/2" h $75

Irishman, papier-mâché, removable head, mkd. "Made in Germany," 7-3/4" h $250

Irishman, papier-mâché on wood base, holding shilleagh, removable head, Germany, 7-1/2" h. $200

Pig, papier-mâché, wooden legs, black, opening in stomach, Germany, 3-1/2" l $95

Top hat, cardboard, green foil, shamrock and clay pipe on top, mkd. "Germany," 3" h $60

Flat Decorations

Carnations with ribbon-tied shamrocks in the background, green and white, mkd., "1964, Eureka, S.P. Co., Scranton, Pa., U.S.A.," 5-1/2" h $8

Harp with shamrocks in the background, cardboard, yellow and green, mkd. "Made in USA," 7" h. . $6

Irish boy dancing, cardboard, green, 11" h $7

Irish girl with green top hat, dancing, cardboard, green and black dress, mkd. "Dennison, USA, 05S," 7" h $10

Irish girl with red hair, dancing, cardboard, green with shamrocks on skirt, mkd., "Dennison, USA, 05S," 7" h. $10

Leprechaun, cardboard, metal grommet at joints of arms and legs, holding hat in hand, green, white and gold, mkd. "Beistle Co., Made In USA," 1960s, 27" h $18

Leprechaun riding a goat, cardboard, printed in green and white, mkd. "Made in USA," 1950s, 15" h. $15

Leprechaun with white hair, surrounded by toadstools and shamrocks, cardboard, shades of green, mkd., "Eureka-U.S.A."
7" h $10
11-3/4" h $15

Pair, Irish boy and girl, boy playing concertina, girl dancing, cardboard, green with various color details, mkd. "Printed in USA," each 7" h $12

Candy/nut cups, crepe paper with foil and cardboard decorations, mkd. "K-Line Party Favors by Kupper Favor Co., Peru, Indiana," 4" h, ea. $3

Pipe tied with ribbons, shamrocks in the background, cardboard, green and white, mkd. "1964 Eureka S.P. Co., Scranton, Pa., USA," 7" h . . $8
Pipe tied with ribbons, shamrocks in the background, cardboard, green and white, mkd. "Made in USA," 4" h $5
Top hat with green flag with harp, cardboard, green and yellow, mkd. "Made in USA," 4" h $5

Figures

Pig

Papier-mâché, black, flocked, 1-1/2" l $15
Papier-mâché, green, flocked, Germany, 1-1/2" h .$25
Papier-mâché, green, flocked, Germany, 4" l . . $40
Papier-mâché, green, flocked, Germany, 6" l . . $65

Miscellaneous

Ball, green and white tissue paper honeycomb, folds-out, 8" d. $4

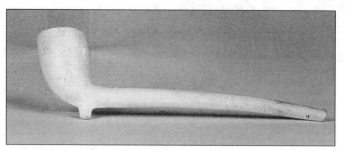

Clay pipe, white, mkd. "TD" on bowl, 6" l $22

Flag, green silk, "Erin Go Bragh" marked on flag with picture of a harp and shamrocks, green painted wood pole with gold finial, 10-1/2" x 7-1/2" . . $25

Pinback Button

"Erin Go Bragh," American Flag and a green flag with harp crossed at the pole, shamrock, celluloid on metal, mkd. "Badge and Novelty Co., Baltimore, Md., 1" d $15

Postcards

Shamrock coming out of envelope, shilleagh in background, 1912 . . . . $3
Four leaf shamrock with familiar Irish sites in each leaf, mkd. "B.P.C. 2411," 1914 . . . . $4
White top hat, shilleagh and clay pipe, mkd. "Series 608," 1911. . . . . $3
Irish gent standing on the letter "17," mkd. "The A.M. Davis Co., Quality Cards, Series 507, Boston," 1912. . . . . $3
"St. Patrick's Day Greeting," shamrock with idyllic scene, clay pipe and black top hat, 1910 . . . . $4
"St. Patrick's Day Greeting, Erin Go Bragh," mkd. "M.B. 200," 1909 . . . . $3

Candy box, tin, green, mkd. "Tindeco, Made in USA," 4" d $35

Candy box, cardboard, USA, 8-1/2" h $30

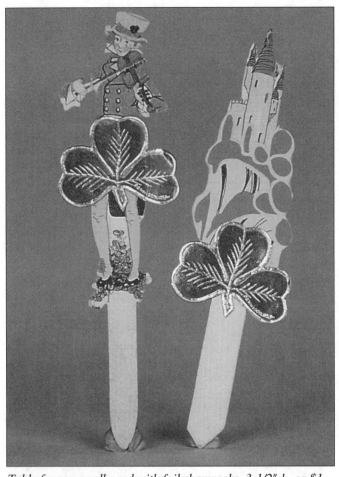

Table favors, cardboard with foil shamrocks, 3-1/2" h, ea.$1

Flat decoration, hat and harp, green cardboard, mkd. "Made in USA," 7-1/2" h $5

Flat decoration, shamrock and clay pipe, cardboard, mkd. "Made in USA," 7" h $4

Flat decoration, leprechaun, cardboard, 10" h $7

Flat decoration , four cardboard shamrocks, mkd. "Made in USA," 2" to 8-1/2" h, set $15

Flat/three-dimensional, cardboard "Erin Go Bragh," green and yellow, green tissue paper honeycomb shamrock, 8-1/2" h $15

Flat/three-dimensional, cardboard green shamrock with green tissue paper honeycomb base, mkd., "H. E. Luhn, Made in USA," 9-1/2" h $18

Two composition pigs, pink, Germany, L: 6-1/2" l $55; R: 5" l $45

Flat decoration, girl dancing, cardboard, hand missing, mkd. "Dennison, USA," 16" h $25

Three-dimensional, green tissue paper honeycomb tophat, mkd. "USA," 10" h $22

Flat/three-dimensional, green cardboard harp and shamrocks with green tissue paper honeycomb base, mkd. "Made in USA," 8-1/2" h $9

Pin, hard plastic, green shamrock and white pipe with green cloth ribbon, 3" l $8

Irish boy, bisque, nodder, green, mkd. "Germany," 2-3/4" h $60

Irish man, green hard plastic with yellow pipe in mouth and yellow cane in hand, 3-3/4" h $10

Postcards, L: mkd. "International Art Publishing Co"; R: mkd. "St. Patrick's Series No. 10," 1914 $5 ea

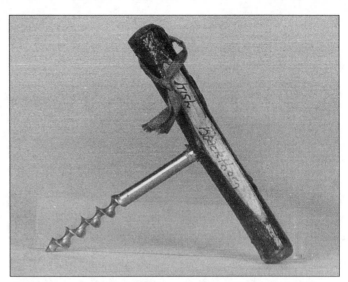

Corkscrew, wood and metal, green satin ribbon, 5" h $18

Prayer card, "St. Patrick of Ireland," mkd. "Made in Italy," 4" h $5

Die-cut, mkd. "L&B, Germany," 3-1/2" h $16

Magazine cover, LIFE, March 13, 1924 $15

CHAPTER 3

EASTER

Easter and spring are synonymous. Between March 22 and April 25th, a specific Sunday is selected based on astronomy (after the first full moon following the vernal equinox). A celebration of rebirth has always been a part of mankind. Cultures from Java to Mexico celebrated the increasing length of the day and the beginning of the growing season. A rite common to many cultures is the practice of lighting fires on hilltops welcoming the sun. With Christianity's rise, the spring festival took on new meaning. The resurrection of Christ was combined with the sun's rebirth and became the holiest day in Western cultures.

The origin of the word Easter is attributed to a derivation of the Saxon Eostre, the goddess of spring. Legend tells of Eostre opening the gates of Valhalla to admit the sun god Baldur, who was murdered. The connection between the rising of the sun in the east and Easter cannot be dismissed.

Common symbols of Easter are the egg and the rabbit. Traditional practices include the sunrise Christian church service on Easter Sunday, the arrival of the Easter rabbit and the egg hunt. The egg has been an important symbol to cultures throughout the world. To the egg was attributed the world's creation, and therefore, it was used as a symbol for fertility and rebirth. The coloring of eggs appears to have originated in the Near East. These early practices were incorporated by the Christian church. Eggs were forbidden during Lent and the egg's appearance on Easter morning symbolized the Lenten season's end.

Two games with eggs were imported to America from Europe. One, the Easter egg roll, began as a contest to roll the eggs down a hill without cracking the shells. The egg rolling game is also frequently linked to rolling the stone away from Christ's tomb. A second, the egg hunt, is held in public parks and homes with either special prize eggs hidden with the others or a prize given for the most eggs found.

The ever popular Easter rabbit is historically a different species. The correct animal for the spring festival, as a symbol of rebirth and a symbol of the

Three baskets, L-R, reed with pink and yellow highlights, mkd. "Japan," 5" h $12; homemade, USA, 13" h $20; reed, mkd. "Germany," repaired with string, 5-1/2" h $15

Spring goddess Eostre, is the hare. The Germans brought the combination of the Easter hare and colored eggs to this country. The Christkindl bringing gifts at Christmas is mirrored by the Easter rabbit bringing colored eggs. Although they are different species most people use the word rabbit and hare interchangeably.

The majority of the Easter symbols represent new life, or a change from death to life, such as the season Spring. Easter collectibles over the decades have focused on the same popular figures. Rabbits, chicks, ducks, decorated eggs, and baskets have been manufactured to decorate homes since the turn of the century.

Baskets

Cane and grass, round, no handle, natural, Germany, 6" d. $8

Cane and rattan, stained dark brown, with row of handpainted multicolored flowers, paper label on base mkd. "Germany," 17" h $25

Cane and woven reed, pink, green and natural, handle, filled with old "grass," Germany, 8" h . . . $15

Books

Easter, compiled by Susan Tracy Rice, Dodd, Mead & Co., New York, 1939 . . . . $7

Candy Containers

Cardboard box with rocking duck ends, lithographed, multicolored, mkd. "Ertel Bros. Co.," Williamsport, PA, USA," 6" l $25

Chick, cloth covered, glass eyes, metal feet, yellow, head removes for candy, 7" h $85

Egg, cardboard covered in gold lithographed paper with red trim, separates in middle, mkd. "container made in Western Germany," 5" l $20

Egg, lithographed tin, yellow, blue, pink and purple, separates in middle, 4" l $10

Egg, molded cardboard, divides in half, gold dresden trim, mkd. "Germany," 3" l $45

Hen on nest, molded cardboard, brown with yellow, red and purple highlights, labeled "Copyright 1924 – F.N. Burt Company, Ltd., Buffalo, NY," 10" h . . $90

Mallard and two ducklings, composition on round cardboard candy box, mkd. "Germany," 5" h $125

Mother Rabbit, plaster, basket of eggs on arm, bottom opens, mkd. "Germany," 6" h $35

Figures

Chicks

Celluloid, yellow and red, mkd. "Japan," 1-1/2" h $15

Cotton batting, yellow, paper covered wire legs and feet, cardboard beak,1-1/2" h $12

Cotton batting, yellow, paper covered wire legs and feet, wood beak, glass eyes, 4-1/2" h $60

Egg

Blown milk glass, handpainted green and pink flowers and leaves and "Easter" in gold, 3-1/2" h $30

Rabbit

Celluloid, ears attached by elastic, white with colored highlights, paper label, mkd. "Japan," 3-1/2" h $55

Composition, white, painted eyes, stamped "Germany" on base, 5" h $90

Cotton batting, white, holding orange carrot, paper label mkd. "Made in Japan," 4-1/2" h. $45

Egg-crate cardboard, brown, glass eyes, 7" h. . $80

Papier-mâché, white with brown highlights, glass eyes, standing on hind feet, 10" h $50

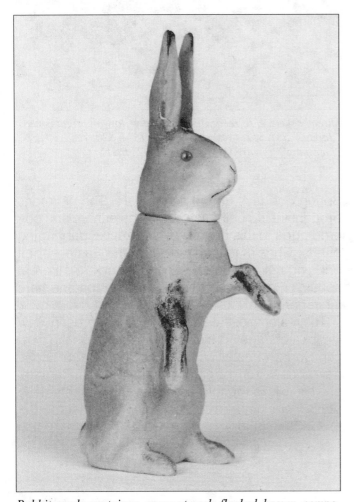

Rabbit candy container, opens at neck, flocked, brown, composition, glass eyes, mkd. "Germany." 10" h $85

Chick, candy container, removable head, yellow flannel coat, metal feet, glass eyes, 1-3/4" h $22

Pressed molded cardboard, pink, head mounted on spring, holding cotton batting carrot, velvet ears with wire reinforcements, pipe cleaner arms, mkd. "Japan," 6" h $12

Greeting Cards

"An Easter Gift," folded, white rabbit sitting in flowers, dated 1914, 4-3/4" h $10

"Easter Greetings, easel back, children swinging and holding rabbits, Howland Greeting Card Co., USA, 3-1/4" h. $4

"Easter Greetings," homemade, cardboard, gold lettering, ink sketch of flowers, dated 1910, flat, 4" h $5

"Good Wishes At Easter," mechanical ears move on small rabbit, easel back, 1960, mkd. "A-Meri-Card, Made in USA," 4" h $4

"Hello There, A Happy Easter," art deco, "child rabbit" among flowers, flat, dated 1932, 4" l $7

"In the Storm – Wishing you every Easter Blessing," child riding waves in boat, flat, cardboard with cloth fringe, 4-1/2" h. $4

"Under Way – May you have a Happy Easter," two boys riding in an egg sailboat, flat, 4-1/2" l . . . $3

Postcards

"A Happy Easter, two children holding a hat full of chicks while mother hen looks on $4

"A Happy Easter," two rabbits painting a rabbit portrait on an egg, 1912 . . . . $5

"A Peaceful Easter," little girl with arm around white rabbit in front of a nest of colored eggs, 1911 . $5

"Easter Greeting," two children stealing a pair of rabbits' Easter eggs while the rabbits hug, mkd. "A.S.B. No. 285, Made in Germany," 1910 . . . $4

"Easter Greetings," three chicks, one wearing top hat, one wearing apron and one carrying big egg, mkd. "International Art Pub. Co., Series No. 2200" $5

"Loving Easter Greetings," two rabbits painting eggs, one wearing glasses, 1914 . . . . $4

"To Wish You A Happy Easter," peeking out of a package, mkd. "Raphael Tuck and Sons, Easter Postcards, Series No. 700, Printed in Saxony" $6

Toy

Chicken house, wood and composition, when door opens the chick pops out, "Germany," 8" d . . $65

Rabbit

Hard plastic, pink, standing upright holding carrot on wheels, mkd. "Made in Hong Kong," 4-1/2" h $15

Lithographed tin, pushing cart, wooden wheels, mkd, "J. Chein and Co., made in USA," 5-1/2" h . . .$80

Wind-up, riding a donkey, metal, rubber and hard plastic, covered in cloth, brown donkey, white rabbit, donkey hops around when wound, mkd. on paper label on donkey, "Made in Japan," 7-1/2" h $45

Egg, molded cardboard, divides in half, mkd. "Made in Germany," 4-1/2" l $60

Egg, candy container, lithographed tin, opens in middle, 6-1/2" l $35

Rabbit candy container, brown molded cardboard, opening in base, mkd. "Germany," 4" d $55

L-R: Chick, cotton batting in composition egg, wire feet, wood beak, paper label mkd. "made in Japan," 2-1/2" d $18; cotton batting rabbit, paper ears, tucksheer green on carrot, Germany, 3" h $22

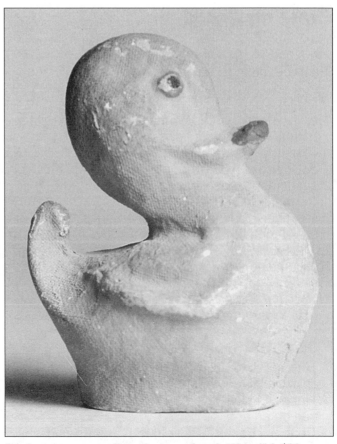

Duck, egg crate cardboard, rose colored, USA, 4" h $30

Rabbit family, pot metal, white, mkd. "Germany," mother 3-1/2" h, babies 1-1/2" h, set $80

Greeting card, easel back, mkd. "Made in USA," 3" h $4

Rabbit, celluloid, mkd. "Japan," 5-1/4" h $35

Rabbit, brown, egg crate cardboard, glass eyes, mkd. "ATCO Co.," USA, 11" h $55

Postcards, L-R, L: mkd. "B.W. Easter, Printed in Germany," 1910 $3; R; mkd. "Raphael Tuck & Sons, Easter Postcards Series, No.101, Printed in Saxony," 1909 $5

Egg, milk glass, hand-painted, 4-1/4" h $25

Rabbits holding eggs, hard plastic, "Happy Easter" on egg, 4" h $10

Greeting card, booklet style, mkd. "C.E.G., Made in USA," 5" h $8

Greeting card, flat, 3-1/2" h $3

Greeting card, embossed cardboard base with cotton batting chick in real egg half-shell with wire feet, 3" h $45

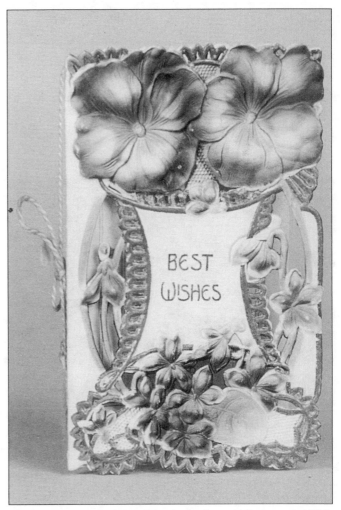

Greeting card, booklet style, embossed purple flowers, 4-1/2" h $15

Rabbit, pink hard plastic, spring toy, 3" h $5

Mrs. Rabbit, missing eyeglasses, yellow, hard plastic, wheels in base, 6"h $12

Metal sled on wheels pulled by celluloid rabbit, wind-up, on the sled is a celluloid swan carrying egg, chick and rabbit, Japan, 9" l $65

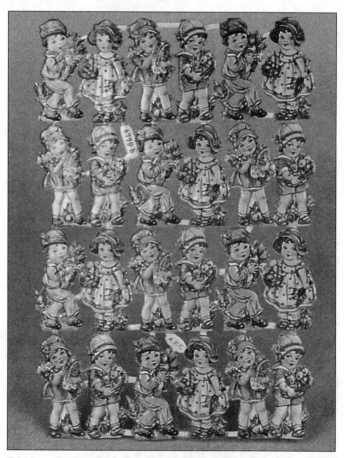

Die-cuts, Easter children, mkd. "A.P.C. 47796, Germany," 9" $22

CHAPTER 4

PATRIOTIC HOLIDAYS

Summer is bracketed by the major patriotic holidays. The warm weather vacation season begins with Memorial Day on May 30th, is centered by Independence Day on July 4th, and ends with Labor Day on the first Monday of September. Memorial Day, also called Decoration Day, is a time set aside to honor those lost in our country's wars. It was established after the Civil War to honor the dead from the North and the South. Waterloo, New York, is credited as the birthplace of this holiday. Boalsburg, Pennsylvania; Columbus, Mississippi; and Belle Isle, Virginia also claim this holiday. Memorial Day has grown to include honoring the dead of our country's wars and also as a time of remembrance of departed family members and friends.

On July 4, 1776, the Declaration of Independence was signed and the United States of America was born. Various colonies had approved of independence from Great Britain and the idea had been debated in the Continental Congress. On June 7, 1776, Richard Henry Lee of Virginia proposed, "That these United Colonies are, and of right ought to be, free and independent States...." Many delegates still were not in favor of a complete separation from England. As a result, a vote on this resolution was delayed. In anticipation of its' approval, a committee was appointed to write a formal statement of Independence. Largely written by Thomas Jefferson, the Declaration of Independence was presented to Congress on July 2, 1776, and signed and published on July 4, 1776.

From the beginning, this special day has been celebrated. Popular activities include parades, public speeches, band concerts and picnics. Fireworks traditionally close this birthday celebration. Red, white and blue banners and bunting started to show up along Main Street, USA in the Victorian era. The Victorians took great pride in their homes and their country and combined the two passions to create elaborate displays of patriotism on their front porches. Many of these decorations have survived and are used to drape the homes of collectors.

The first Monday in September closes the summer season with the celebration of Labor Day. The first Labor Day parade sponsored by the Central Labor Union of New York City was held in 1882. In 1894, President Grover Cleveland signed a bill legalizing this holiday in the District of Columbia.

Labor Day honors not only those whose work fueled the Industrial Revolution and the growth of this country, but the concept that through work, success may be obtained. Today, Labor Day is an important family day noted by picnics, travel and sporting events.

Additional patriotic holidays include President's Day, Flag Day, and Veteran's Day. President's Day was originally two separate holidays for the majority of the nation: Abraham Lincoln's Birthday on February 12th and George Washington's Birthday on February 22nd. In a Federal law passed in 1968, Washington's birthday celebration was moved to the third Monday in February. This law was passed to give Federal workers a three-day weekend and eventually was adopted by all the states. The same law also moved Memorial Day from actually being celebrated on May 30th to the last Monday in May.

George Washington candy container, bisque figure with crepe paper clothing, metal axe, homemade, circa 1920s, 6-1/2" h
$200

"The Man Without A Country" by Edward Everett Hale, 1925, Little, Brown & Co., 1925 $10

Abraham Lincoln's Birthday was first celebrated in 1866, the year after his assassination, with a small ceremony in Washington D.C. After that, the holiday grew in popularity until the majority of the states celebrated this day. Several southern states never officially recognized the holiday. However, to most of the nation, President's Day recognizes both Washington and Lincoln and is celebrated on the third Monday in February. The majority of the decorations for Lincoln's birthday were centered around school and store displays. Flat cutouts of President Lincoln and of log cabins are popular themes. Postcards and magazine covers frequently featured Lincoln and Civil War themes.

Different cities and organizations celebrated George Washington's birthday sporadically during his lifetime. Washington's birthday gained national acceptance on the centennial of his birth in 1832. The celebration gained in popularity. Tall tales about his childhood also became larger than life. The celebrated story about chopping down the cherry tree and admitting to it, because he could

not tell a lie, was a lie, a complete fabrication! Amazingly, that myth became so popular that the majority of the holiday collectibles associated with his birthday feature part of that story. Washington's Birthday candy containers, both at the turn of the century and through the early part of the twentieth century, were often logs covered with cherries, or cardboard axes stuffed with candy. Postcards frequently picture the bust of Washington with cherry decorations.

On June 14, 1777, a resolution by the Continental Congress described the flag that was to become a symbol of the new nation. It was to have thirteen alternating red and white stripes and thirteen white stars in a blue field. The number thirteen was in honor of the thirteen original colonies. There has never been any official verification of the Betsy Ross legend. Betsy Ross was a flag-making seamstress that lived in Philadelphia, but there are no records of Betsy Ross making the first American flag. Over the years the anniversary of the flag resolution was celebrated by patriotic speeches and flag displays. It was not officially recognized until 1949, when Congress passed the National Flag Day Bill and President Truman signed the holiday into history. June 14th does not usually inspire large parades and community celebrations, but people do usually display the flag and occasionally drape their porches and stores in patriotic bunting.

Veteran's Day was originally known as Armistice Day. November 11th was designated as Armistice Day, because WWI ended on the eleventh month, on the eleventh day, at the eleventh hour. The day honored those who gave their lives for their country during World War I. Over the next several decades, the United States survived two more wars, World War II and The Korean War. Consequently, Congress in 1954, passed a bill that changed Armistice Day to Veteran's Day and made it a day that honored all veterans on November 11th each year. President Eisenhower signed the bill. Congress made one more change to the holiday with the 1968 bill that changed the celebration of Veteran's Day to the fourth Monday in October. However, to many Americans Veteran's Day will always be November 11th. Postcards and paper memorabilia dominate the Veteran's Day collectibles.

Banner

Silk, "We Can—We Will—We Must," Franklin D. Roosevelt, white background two American flags, a star, wings, and a propeller; red, white and blue with gold fringe on the bottom, 12"x18-1/2" . . $50

Small paper American flags strung on red and white braided string, paper label mkd. "Old Glory Streamer," 24" l $20

Book

Flag Day, edited by Robert Haven Schauffler, part of Our American Holidays Series, Dodd, Mead and Company, New York, NY, 1912. . . . . $7

Independence Day, edited by Robert Haven Schauffler, part of Our American Holidays Series, Dodd, Mead and Company, New York, NY, 1912 . . . $7

School Melodies Songbook, pub. By Taller-Meredith Co., New York, Chicago, 1910, Uncle Sam pictured on cover surrounded by red, white and blue bunting. $8

The Grant Patriotic Book by Lenore Hetrick, Paine Pub. Co., Dayton, Ohio $25

Box

Drum, cardboard, red, white and blue lithographed paper cover, 1920s, 3" h $25

Shield, cardboard, red, white and blue satin, 1920s, 3" h. $20

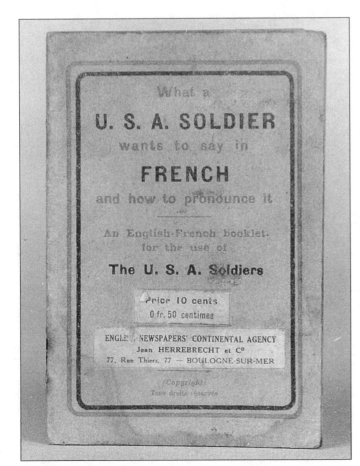

Booklet, World War I, 5" h $15

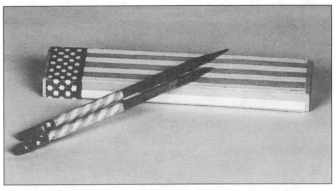

Pencil box, cardboard, slate pencils, box 5-1/2" l, set $30

Bunting

Cloth, red, white and blue, blue areas have white stars, circa 1930, 16' l $70

Candy Container

Box, cardboard, red, white and blue with metal cannon on top, 1920s, 4" d $45

Bust of George Washington, papier-mâché, mkd. "Germany," 4" h $145

George Washington on horse, cloth covered gray horse, head removes from body, Washington has a bisque face, wood hands, cloth clothes, 13" h $550

Hat, cardboard covered with lithographed paper, red, white and blue, Germany, 4-1/2" d $85

Log, cardboard tied with red grosgrain ribbon decorated with red, white and blue ribbons tied with red composition cherry, log slides open to hold candy, mkd. "Japan," 4-1/2" l $65

Tree stump, molded cardboard, brown, red and starred blue medallion with George Washington portrait, mkd. "Germany," 7" h $200

Uncle Sam, cardboard, cylinder, moveable arms, hat band says "Fanny Farmer," USA, 6" h $70

Clothing

Belt, blue cloth with white stars, homemade 1936, 24" l $10

Sash, blue cloth glass beaded silver stars and red and white stripes, circa 1925, 39" l $55

Scarf, red silk, silk-screened "Remember Me, Greetings from Camp Hancock, Augusta, Georgia," from WWI, 17" sq. $25

Skirt, red and white wool stripes sewn together, homemade for parade 1936 . . . . $45

Figure

Uncle Sam, papier-mâché, wood base, red, white and blue with touches of gray, green, yellow and black, moveable arms, mkd. "Germany," 5-1/2" h . . . $300

Uncle Sam, wood-covered with paper, cloth clothing, USA, 10" h $400

Octagonal tin with handle, multicolored, mkd. "Loose-Wiles Biscuit Co., Bakers of Sunshine Biscuit, New York, NY," 9-1/2" wide $25

Newspaper Photo

Children and mother draping flowers over father's Civil War picture, titled "On Memorial Day," supplement to Grit, Williamsport, PA, May 29, 1904 . $12

Pennant

Paper, red, white and blue, "Welcome Home, Well Done My Boys, God Bless You All My Boys and Girls," mkd. "copyrighted 1945, KP Bonter, 30 W. Harrison St., Chicago 5, Illinois, Tel. Webster 7488," 34-1/4" l $35

Pinback Buttons

"Betsy Ross House, Philadelphia, PA," her house pictured flanked by two flags, red, white and blue, celluloid on metal, red, white and blue silk ribbon and metal Liberty Bell attached to pin, mkd. on paper label on back, "Philadelphia Badge Co., Philadelphia, PA," 3/4" d $12

"Labor Day, Labor Omnia Vincit, In Union There Is Strength, Justice For All," two hands shaking, flanked by a red, white and blue shield and an eagle, celluloid on metal, mkd. on paper label on back, "Badge and Novelty Co., Baltimore, Md., design pat'd.," 1" d. $20

Two flags with poles crossed, red silk flag attached to base of celluloid on metal pin, unmarked, 1" d . $10

Postcards

"A Grateful Land Remembers All Her Promises to do," children holding flowers underneath a flag held by a child, mkd. "Raphael Tuck & Sons, Decoration Day Series, No.173, Printed in Saxony," 1908 . $5

"Abraham Lincoln, The Martyred President," Lincoln at lectern, mkd. "1908 by E. Nash, Lincoln Birthday Series No.1" $4

"For Us Their Precious Lives They Gave, For Freedom's Sacred Cause They Died," wife draping patriotic bunting over Civil War veteran's portrait, mkd. "Raphael Tuck & Sons, Decoration Day Series Postcards, No.158, Printed in Saxony, 1910" $5

"Fraternity, Loyalty and Charity," Civil War battle paraphernalia, mkd. "Decoration Series No. 1, 1909" $4

"Lincoln Centennial Souvenir 1809-1909," Lincoln freeing the slaves, mkd. "Copyright 1908, E. Nash, Lincoln Birthday Series No.1, 1909" . . . $3

"My Country 'Tis Of Thee," child dressed as Lady Liberty, mkd. "International Art Pub. Co., 1908"$4

"The Glorious Fourth, waving flag, mkd. "International Art Pub. Co., Series No. 2443, 1911" $4

"The Star Spangled Banner," flag within a flowered wreath, mkd. "Raphael Tuck & Sons, Decoration Day Postcards, Printed in Germany, 1908 . . . $5

"Three Cheers For George Washington," mkd. "International Art Pub. Co., No. 51646, 1909. . . . $4

Octagonal tin with handle, multicolored, White House on lid, portraits of Presidents around the sides with the last President listed as "FDR 1933- , mkd. "Loose-Wiles Biscuit Co., Bakers of Sunshine Biscuit, New York, NY," 9-1/2" wide $25

Hat, Milan straw, 1920s, 5" h $45

Bow-tie, cloth, part of parade costume, 1930s, 7" l $10

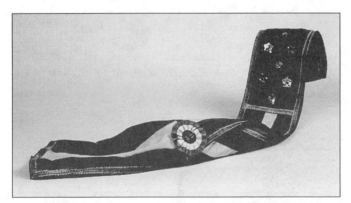

Sash, velvet, red and white stripes, blue velvet has silver stars with bullion stitches, 39-1/2" l $40

Log stumps with cherries and hatchet, cardboard with composition cherries, mkd. "Japan," 5" h $75

Parasol, paper top, bamboo spokes and handle, mkd. "Germany," 3' d when opened $70

Toy soldiers, pot metal, World War I, 2" h $10 ea.

Candy/nut cups, crepe paper, tissue paper and cardboard, mkd. "C. A. Reed Product, C. A. Reed, Williamsport, PA," 4" h $4 ea.

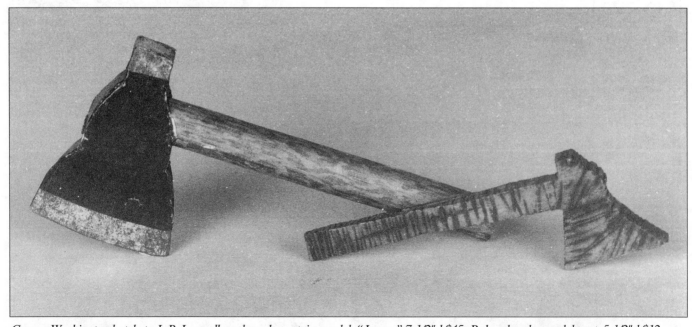

George Washington hatchets, L-R, L: cardboard candy container, mkd. "Japan," 7-1/2" l $45; R: handmade wood, burnt, 5-1/2" l $12

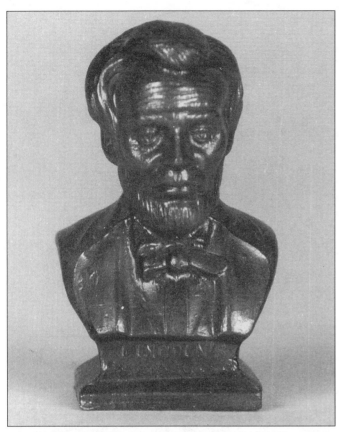

Bust of Abraham Lincoln, metal, mkd. "Illinois Pavillion, New York World's Fair, 1967," 3" h $12

Statue of Liberty, pot metal, 4-1/2" h $15

Eagle, metal, 6" h $45

Liberty Bells, L: bank, mkd. "Danville National Bank, manuf. By The Bankers Saving & Credit System Co., Cleveland, OH, USA, pat'd. Feb 19, 1919" $40; R: mkd. "1776-1962," 1-1/4" h $10

Soldier, celluloid, paper label mkd. "Made in Japan," 6-1/2" h $35

George Washington hatchets, table favors, cardboard, USA, 3" l $1 ea.

Flag, silk, red, white, blue with black, 7-1/2"x12" $30

Flags, L: Cotton, 48 stars, wood pole, gold finial, 10" h; R: Silk, with gold fringe, 48 stars, wood pole, 10" h $10 ea.

Top, metal, red, white and blue, mkd. "Gibbs Toy," 3" h $35

Fan, cardboard, pull-out, mkd. "Made In USA, No. 36, Pat#1655229," 7-1/2" h $10

Lantern, paper and wood, mkd. "Germany," 9-1/2" h $60

Fan, cardboard, mkd. "Bud The Tailor, Joseph Morris Co., Youngstown, OH," 9-3/4" h $18

Fan, cardboard with wood handle, mkd. "Courogen's Luncheonette, Danville, PA," 14" h $25

Place card, cardboard, mkd. "Made in USA," 2-3/4" h $2

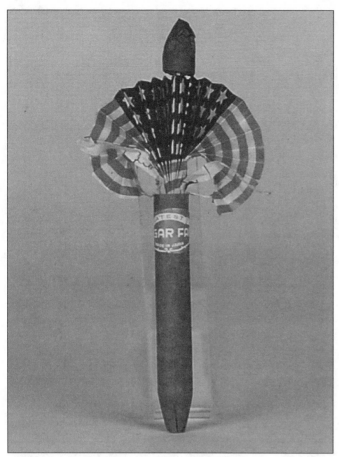

Cigar fan, cardboard cigar, when pulled apart tissue paper flag appears, mkd. "made in Japan," 4" l closed $40

Hat, cardboard, with tissue paper honeycomb interior mkd. "George Washington's 200th Anniversary, 1732-1932, Made in US Amer." 11-1/2" l $40

Three-dimensional decoration, tissue paper honeycomb, 17" d, open $10

CHAPTER 5

HALLOWEEN

Halloween is the one holiday for kids of all ages to just have fun. Halloween decorations are one of the most popular with collectors. Celebrated on October 31st, it is a time for pleasant scariness, tricks, costumes and candy.

The antecedents of present-day Halloween are the fall harvest festivals and the eve of the New Year in the old pagan calendar. To the Celtic people, who followed the Druid religion, November 1st was New Year's Day and the day marking the beginning of winter with the returning of cattle to the barns.

As with most old festivals, fire was an important part of this holiday. At this time, household fires were allowed to go out and were rekindled from a sacred fire. This holiday was also a time to remember the dead. Fires provided a greeting to returning souls and protection from ghosts and witches.

New Year's fires were also used to foretell the future. Stones, vegetables and nuts were thrown into the heat, and how they reacted forecast the next twelve months. An outgrowth of this practice was to hollow out large vegetables such as turnips and illuminate them with candles. These vegetables were the ancestors of our jack-o'-lantern.

Today's custom of Halloween costumes and children going door to door "trick or treating" also heralds from the pre-Christian practices of the November 1st festival welcoming the new year. It was believed that the souls of the dead returned at this time and they were welcomed with a feast. At the end of the feast, villagers in costumes representing these souls led the ghosts out of the village with dancing and a parade.

Jack-o'-lantern lanterns trio, papier-mâché, L-R, 7" h, 5-1/2" h, 5" h $110 to $50

Christianity hallowed this October 31st-November 1st festival by moving All Saints Day to this date. It was a universal day to celebrate the lives of the church's saints, whether recognized or not.

Avid collectors eagerly seek Halloween artifacts and decorations today. Second in popularity only to Christmas, many collectors display their Halloween decorations all year long. Items made from numerous materials include ghosts, skeletons, pumpkins, witches, bats, owls and black cats.

Halloween parades have been popular for decades in many communities throughout the country. The costumes and masks worn in parades and for "trick or treating" are also valued by Halloween antique buffs. Arranged on a wall, they bring back memories for some and generate new memories for others.

Banner

Jack-o'-lanterns, crepe paper, horizontal design, orange on black, 20" w x 10' l $40
Pumpkin man & black cats, crepe paper, vertical design, orange, yellow & black, 6" w x 10' l $45

Book

Dennison Bogie Book, 1917, Dennison Paper Co. $40
Halloween, Our American Holiday Series, Dodd, Mead and Co., 1912 . . . . $8
The Great Halloween Book, by Lenore Hetrick, Paine Pub. Co., Dayton, Ohio $25

Candles

Black cat by white candle, mkd. on base, "Gurley Candle Co., Buffalo, NY," 4" h $4
Haunted house, orange, mkd. "Capri Candle Co., 6" h. $8
Pumpkin, orange, 2-1/2" h. $4
Set, dozen Halloween candles, box marked "Made in Japan" $25
Witch with cat at side, orange & black, 3" h $3

Candy Container

Black cat, cloth covered composition, glass eyes, black, removable head, 7" h $300

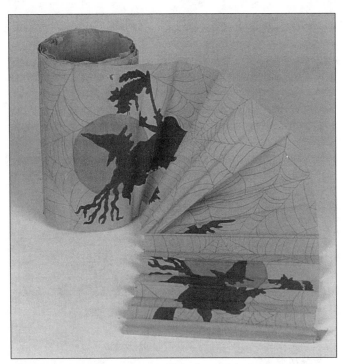

Banner, orange crepe paper w/black witches, horizontal design, 15' l $45

Black cat, composition, sitting on round cardboard box, 4" h. $175

Black cat dressed as a girl, composition, removable head, black, orange, green and white, Germany, 4" h. $165

Black cat, sitting, egg crate cardboard, opening in bottom, black and white, Germany, 9" h . . . $175

Box, lithographed cardboard, oval with handle, multicolored with printed Halloween figures all over box, 3" l $38

Box, lithographed cardboard, rectangular with cardboard handle, orange and black, 4' l $30

Cat and jack-o'-lantern lollypop holder, hard plastic, orange and black, 3" h. $20

Jack-o'-lantern head with black witch hat, removable hat, molded paper and cardboard, orange and black, 5" h $70

Jack-o'-lantern man, painted glass, Jeanette Candy Co., 5" h. $400

Mushroom shaped box with face, molded cardboard, beige and brown, mushroom cap opens, 4" h $60

Pumpkin figure with pumpkin head and a pumpkin body, composition, yellow, mkd. "Germany," 4" h $145

Round box with ghost face, cardboard, brown and white, 3-3/4" h $45

Skeleton, cardboard and composition skeleton, black and white, opens on bottom, 4" h. . . . $185

Vegetable head person, composition, cardboard and crepe paper, removable head, green and brown, 5" h. $250

Witch holding pumpkin, hard plastic, orange and black, 1950s, 3-3/4" h $20

Witch riding bicycle with jack-o'-lantern riding on back, hard plastic, orange, black and green, "pops" wrapped in cellophane in jack-o'-lantern and handle bars, 1950s, 5" l $35

Witch riding broom, hard plastic, orange and black, candy holder, 1950s, 5-1/2" h $20

Witch riding rocket, hard plastic, orange and black, "pops" were in fuel jets of rocket, 1950s, 5" l. $30

Witch with jack-o'-lantern face, composition and cardboard, black and orange, straw hair, opens in base, 5" h $200

Costumes

Black cat, cloth one-piece black and yellow costume, plastic face, original box, child's medium 8-10, box mkd. "Halloween Costume, Made in USA" . . $22

Bride, dress and veil, original box, child's medium 8-10, Halco Superior Brand, J. Halpern Co., Pittsburgh, PA. $20

Casper, "Collegeville," painted cloth with plastic mask, original box, child's small 4-6, 1960s . $25

Clown, homemade, cloth, brown and gold one-piece suit with "pom-pom" button made from shredded cloth, pointed cardboard hat covered with gold cloth and small gold bells, 1940s. $65

Mickey Mouse, cloth with plastic face, original box, child, box mkd. "Walt Disney Character Costume, Ben Cooper Inc., N.Y." $55

Book, "Halloween Frolic," David C. Cook Publishing Co., Elgin, Ill., 1908 $20

Prince Phillip, painted cloth shirt and pants, felt hat with feather, plastic belt and mask, original box, child's medium 8-10, box mkd. "Walt Disney Character Costume, Ben Cooper Inc., N.Y." $30
Skeleton, one-piece black and white cloth suit, white gauze mask, child's large 12-14, 1950s $20
Tinker Bell, homemade, yellow, pink and green, crepe paper, plastic mask, child's size, 1950s $20
Witch, black cloth with yellow highlights, dress and short cape, no mask, child's large 12-14, paper label mkd. "All Rayon, Bland Charnas, Co., Inc., USA" $15
Witch, homemade, orange, black and yellow crepe paper, adult, 1950s $70

Fan

Flat, cardboard with wood handle, cat dancing at a Halloween party pictured on fan, orange, yellow and black, 1920s, 10" h $55
Wood and paper, black cat on orange background, 10" open. $45

Figure

Black cat, chenille "stick" body, cotton batting head, stands on back feet, 5-1/2" h $25
Comic pumpkin face with stem, papier-mâché, orange, 13" h $250
Jack-o'-lantern nodder, composition, orange, black and red, mkd. "Made in Germany," 4" h. . . . $200

Book, "Proud Pumpkin" by Nora S. Unwin, Aladdin Book, New York, 1953 $18

Candle, girl dressed as witch, orange and black, mkd. 12 cents, 3-1/2" h $7

Pumpkin, orange honeycomb tissue paper, green and brown heavy stock paper stem, mkd. "Made in U.S.A.," 1960s, 10" d open $20
Scarecrow, straw with crepe paper clothing, mkd. "Japan," 6" h $45
Vegetable head figure, celluloid, multicolored, 3-1/2" h $75
Witch, cardboard and tissue paper, with wooden broom, orange and black, paper label mkd. "Made in Occupied Japan," 5" h $40
Witch riding a motorcycle, hard plastic, orange and black, 7" h $35

Flat Decorations

Cat musicians, set of 3, embossed cardboard, orange and black, mkd. "Germany," 10" h . . . $165
Devil, cardboard, red, articulated arms, legs and tail, 10" h $30
Jack-o'-lantern pumpkin, cardboard, orange and black, 5-1/4" h $15
Owl, embossed cardboard, black with yellow and white, mkd. "Germany." 15" h $45
Party favor, cat head, cardboard, black, "fortune" on back, mkd. "Dennison," 3" h $8
Silhouette set, construction paper, black, assortment of 10, owls, cats, bats, and witches, 5-1/2" to 8" h $10
Skeleton, cardboard, articulated arms and legs, white on orange, mkd. "Made in USA, Beistle," 24"h $35

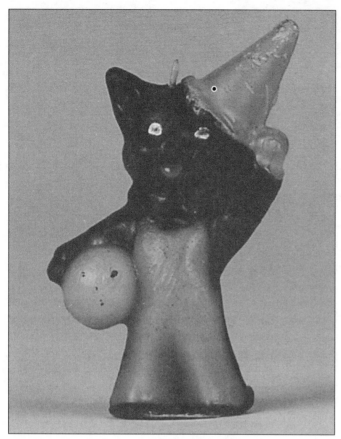

Candle, cat, mkd. "Gurley Novelty Co., Buffalo, NY, USA," 3-1/2" h $8

Hat

Cardboard and honeycomb tissue, scary face on front of hat, multicolored, 6" h $35
Crepe paper, orange with black trim, 9" l $7

Lantern

Devil head, flat cardboard sides connected with tissue paper honeycomb, black & red, 7-1/2" h. $75
Devil head, molded cardboard, red, 4" h $155
Devil head, papier-mâché, 4-1/2" h $250
Four-sided, black cardboard silhouettes with orange tissue paper backing, silhouettes are witches, owls and pumpkins, 6-1/2" h $75
Jack-o'-lantern, flat cardboard sides connected with tissue paper honeycomb, orange, 4-1/4" h . . $40
Jack-o'-lantern, tin, hand-painted, 6-1/2" h . . . $250
Jack-o'-lantern with Japanese lantern hat, molded cardboard, tissue paper features, wire handle, orange, 5" h. $85
Japanese-style lantern, pleated and folded paper, orange with black witch, 8" h $80
Owl, molded cardboard, gray, black and white, wire handle, 5" h $95
Pumpkin head man, papier-mâché, tissue paper features, 7" h. $80

Six-sided, top and bottom, black cardboard, orange tissue paper backing, assorted Halloween figures in cardboard, 8" h $70
Skull head, glass and metal, battery operated, black and white, mkd. "Hong Kong," 5" h $55
Skull head, molded cardboard, white, 3" h $80
Witch, composition, straw broom, multicolored, removable head, Germany, 5" h $190
Witch head, molded cardboard, black and white, 18" h $285
Witch's kettle, comic face, molded cardboard, wire handle, black, 7-1/2" h. $110

Magazine Cover

Child Life, October, 1935, witch and cat riding broom over autumn scene $12
The Farmer's Wife, October, 1929, child in costume carrying pumpkin lantern and escorted by black cat $15
Today's Housewife, October, 1919, child looking through window on Halloween night $20

Mask

Black face, papier-mâché, white circles around eyes, red around mouth, cotton string, mkd. "Germany," 9" l $45

Candy container, witch, papier-mâché, orange with black trim, 8" h $110

Candy container, jack-o'-lantern, hard plastic, metal bail, orange and black, 4" h $35

Clown, white with bright colors, plastic, child's, stamped "Ben Cooper, Inc.," 7" l $8
Devil, red, latex rubber, painted features, 8" l . . $25
Elephant, gray with painted highlights, gauze, small yellow bell sewn on each ear, 8" h $30
Half mask, black cloth, 1950s $7
Half Mask, gray and green, plastic with ruffled plastic trim, stamped 15 cents $4
Man with long side burns, papier-mâché, painted features, mkd. "Germany," 8-1/2" l $35
Werewolf, latex rubber, mkd. "29 cents," 6" l . . . $20

Miscellaneous

Advertisement, "F. W. Woolworth & Co.," 1954, color ad for costumes, masks, candy and toys. $10
Cookie cutters, "Trick or Treat," original box, set of 6—bat, pumpkin, owl, witch, broom and cat . $40
Invitation, jack-o'-lantern surrounded by witches on brooms, mkd. "made in USA" $10
Parasol, open, celluloid, orange and black, 3-1/2" h.$35
Party favor, wine bottle with pumpkin face, molded cardboard, black and orange, mkd. "Germany," 9" h. $130
Party favor, witch on candy box, composition witch, cardboard box, mkd. "Germany," 3" h $75
Sheet music, "Halloween Dance" by H. Engelman, Jos. Morris Co., Phila., 1907 . . . . $40
Tea set for four, child's, hard plastic, orange with jack-o'-lantern faces, mkd. "Hong Kong," cup, 1-1/2" h $65

Tin, black with witch holding pumpkin on cover, small Halloween symbols around edge of tin, 4" d . $95
Trick or Treat bag, lithographed paper, jack-o'-lantern face, orange and black, 12" h $5

Noisemaker

Horn, lithographed cardboard, orange and black, 6-1/2" l $20
Ratchet, pumpkin man riding black cat, wood, composition, crepe paper, mkd. "Germany," 12" l . . .$200
Rattle, jack-o'-lantern, lithographed paper cardboard and wood, orange and green, mkd. "Made in Germany," 3-1/2" h $85
Rattle, skull, paper, crepe paper and wood, black and white, 8" l $110
Saxaphone, molded cardboard, red devil head on stem, 8" l $190
Squeaker, cardboard, "funny face," red and brown, 3" h $50
Tambourine horn, cat on tambourine, cardboard and wood, orange and black, mkd. "Germany," 8" h $70

Postcards

"A Thrilling Halloween," young child frightened by jack-o'-lantern in window,signed, Ellen Clapsaddle $12
"Halloween," children bobbing for apples $6
"Halloween," girl dressed in witch's costume hugging black cat, Raphael Tuck & Sons $9

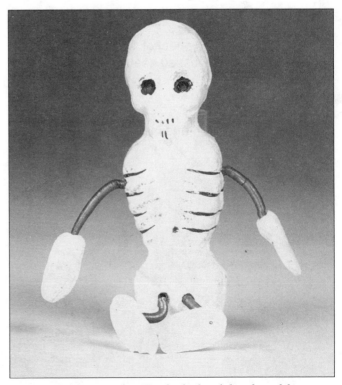

Figure, skeleton, composition body, head, hands and feet, spring wire arms and legs, 4" h $75

Candy holder, scarecrow figure with pumpkin cup on back, hard plastic, orange and black, 5" h $28

"You would laugh too," moon watching witches dance around a jack-o'-lantern $6

Seals

Acorn heads, gummed seals, shades of brown, set of 5, 1" h. $4
Black cats, embossed sheet of 15, Germany . . $85
Jack-o'-lanterns, embossed heavy paper, set of 10, 1" h. $20

Stickpins

Black cat, composition and metal, 1" h $20

Tablecloth, paper, 36" sq. $5

Candy container, jack-o'-lantern, hard plastic, orange and black, 2" h $12

Toy

Jack-in-the-box, witch is papier-mâché, box is paper covered wood, 4" h $350
Pull toy, cat and jack-o'-lantern, hard plastic, on wheels, orange and black, 6-1/2" l $22
Scissor toy, jack-o'-lantern, wood and cardboard, black and orange, mkd. "Japan," 7" h $55
"Spin and Sparkle," made of springs and lithographed tin, cat face, 4" l $40

Candy container, cat, egg crate cardboard, tissue paper features, 7" h $125

Candy nut cups, crepe paper and cardboard, 4-1/2" h $10 ea.

Child's Native American costume, doll holding 1921 photo of child wearing same costume, cloth with leather and bead trim, headdress cloth and feathers, leather moccasins, tag in skirt mkd. "size 4" $85

Figure, jack-o'-lantern holding "black" wood carved figure with cloth trim, jack-o'-lantern is wax covered papier-mâché, dried moss at base, 7-1/2" h $300

Figure, lithographed cardboard black and green scarecrow with yellow honeycomb tissue paper cornstalks and orange honeycomb tissue paper pumpkin, mkd. "Made in USA," 8-1/2" h $30

Figure, cat, cardboard, black, tail connected to head with black honeycomb tissue paper, mkd. "made in USA," 10" h $30

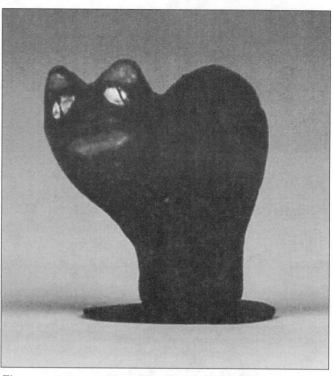

Figure, cat, composition, Germany, 1-1/2" h $45

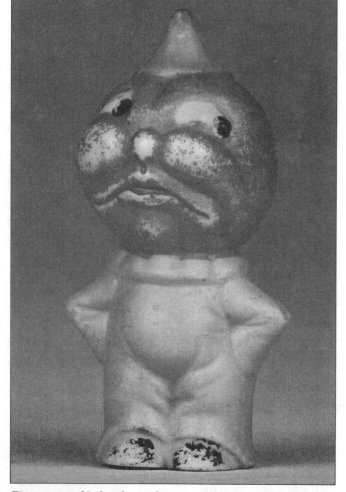

Figure, pumpkin head man, bisque, mkd. "Germany," 3" h $75

Figure, jack-o'-lantern, egg crate papier-mâchè, mkd. "P1Atco Co.," 4-1/2" h $55

Flat decoration, owl in moon, embossed cardboard, mkd. "Germany," 10-1/2" h $70

Flat decoration, doorknob sign, cardboard, orange, yellow and black, 9" h $20

Flat decoration, cat, orange and black construction paper, 9" h $15

Flat decorations, cardboard, original packaging "10 for 10," USA $50

Flat decoration, cat in half moon, embossed cardboard, black and orange, mkd. "Made in USA, Copr. H. E. Luhrs," 20" h $35

Flat decoration, pumpkin man, embossed cardboard, wood base, mkd. "Germany," 3" h $38

Flat decoration, witch riding broom, embossed cardboard, orange and black, mkd. "Germany," 10" h $40

Figure, pumpkin head man, composition, Germany, 2" h $110

Flat decorations, cardboard, owl and jack-o'-lantern, owl is yellow and brown, jack-o'-lantern is orange, paper label mkd. "Dennison, USA," 3" h $3 ea.

Flat decorations, set of three, cardboard, stand-up, mkd. "Printed in USA," 10-1/2" h $15 ea.

Hat, orange crepe paper, orange and black lithograph paper band trim, mkd. "Made in Japan," 8" h $20

Flat decorations, cat, embossed cardboard, mkd. "Germany," black with white and yellow, 15" h $65

Flat decoration, cardboard, witch on pumpkin, 12" h $28

Hat, orange and black crepe paper, black and gold lithograph band, bell on top, 9" h $35

Flat decorations, set, cardboard, double-sided, holes for stringing, 3" h $5 ea.

Jack-o'-lanterns, hard plastic, orange, wire bail, battery light, L- mkd. "Union Products, Inc.,Leominster, Mass," 4" h $40 , R- mkd. "PULPCO, Mill., Wis," 1950s, 4" h $36

Hats, cardboard, orange and black lithograph, largest is 5" h $14, smallest is mkd. "Made in Germany" and is 4" h $28

Hat, cardboard, orange with black cat, mkd. "5 cents," 5" h $18

Jack-o'-lantern, papier-mâché, tissue paper features, wire bail, 5" h $85

Jack-o'-lantern, glass with metal rim and bail, painted features, 4" h $125

Lantern, cat, black and white cardboard, orange tissue paper features, two sides connected with honeycomb tissue paper, 11" h $95

Jack-o'-lantern, papier-mâché, tissue paper features, 5" h $95

Jack-o'-lantern light, orange and black, metal, glass and hard plastic, battery operated, mkd, "Made In Japan," 8" h $65

Jack-o'-lantern, molded cardboard, tissue paper feature, Germany, metal bail, 4" h $130

Lantern, two sided, witch silhouette on one side and a bat and a cat on the other side, cardboard and tissue paper, mkd. "Made in U.S. AM.," 11" h $100

Jack-o'-lantern, papier-mâché, wire bail, 4" h $70

Lantern, cat, papier-mâché, wire bail, mkd. "PULP Reproduction Co., Mil., Wis., Made in USA," 7" h $85

Jack-o'-lantern, tin, orange, black, green and white, mkd. "U.S. Metal Toy Manuf. Co., Made in USA," 4-1/2" h $65

Lantern, cat, molded cardboard, tissue paper features, wire bail, Germany, 4" h $130

Magazine cover, Saturday Evening Post, *November 2, 1935 $18*

Magazine cover, People's Popular Monthly, *October 1930 $15*

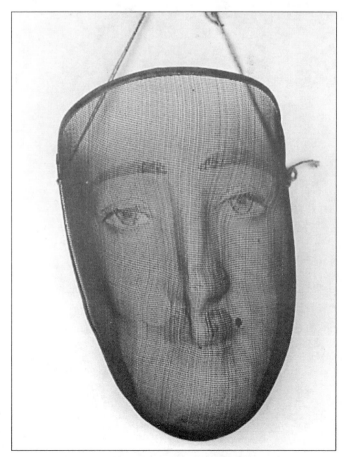

Mask, painted metal screen, string tie, 8" h $95

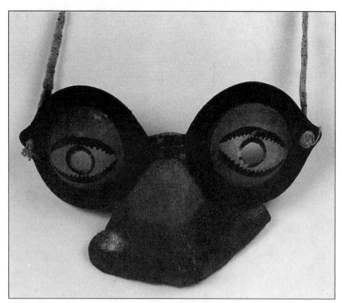

Mask, glasses and nose, papier-mâché, painted features, mkd. "Germany," 3-1/2" h $28

Mask, clown, gauze, 7" h $22

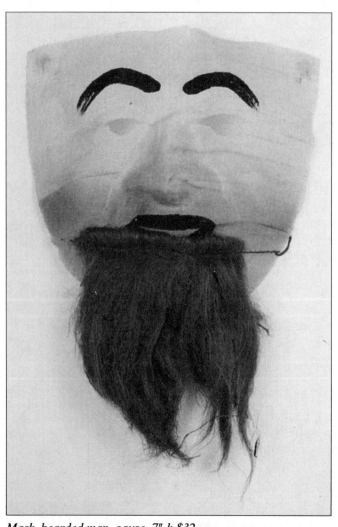

Mask, bearded man, gauze, 7" h $32

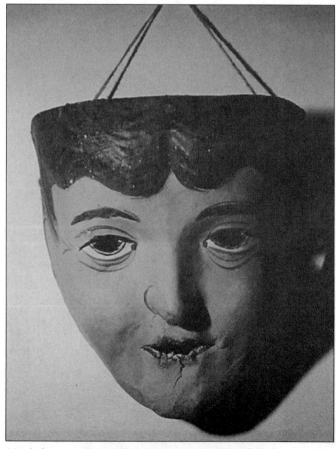

Mask, boy, papier-mâché, Germany, 7-1/2" h $42

Photograph, 1943, 5"x7" $25

"Witches Mystery Answer Game," cardboard, orange and black, easel back, mkd. "Made in U.S. AM., $55

Pair of Griffin candlesticks, black, metal, 5-1/2" h $50 pr.

Whirl O'Halloween Fortune and Stunt Game, cardboard, metal spinner, mkd. "Made in USA" $60

Homemade decorations, construction paper, 1940s $5 ea.

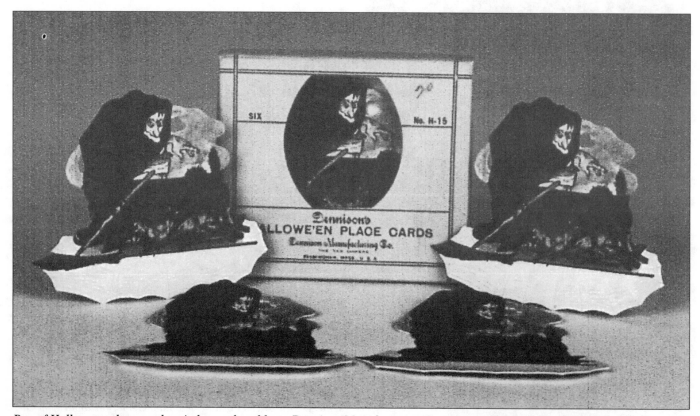

Box of Halloween place cards, witches and cauldron, Dennison Manufacturing Co., Framingham, Mass., USA, 3" h $40

Photograph, October 30, 1948, 8"x10" $20

Pack of napkins, 36 ct., mkd. "A Reed Product, manuf. By C.A. Reed Co., Williamsport, PA., USA" $5

Owl, homemade, stuffed, black crepe paper with painted gold dots, gold cardboard beak and button eyes, 1930s, 7" h $32

Tambourine with a cat head, lithographed tin orange, black and white, mkd. "T. Cohn Inc., Made in USA," 7" d $55

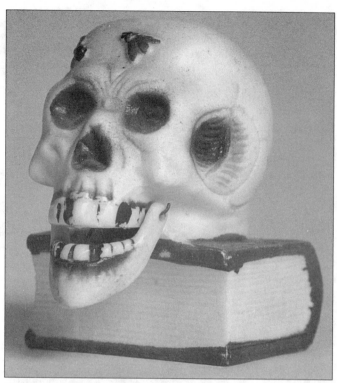

Skull on book, moveable jaw, bisque, mkd. "Made in Japan," 3" h $50

Trick or Treat bag, paper, orange, black and white, 7" h $1

Gargoyle candlestick, black, metal, 6" h $30

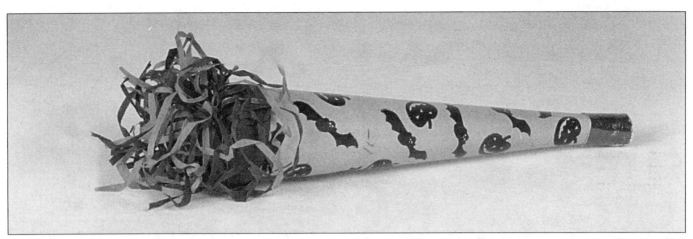

Horn, cardboard with crepe paper trim, orange and black, mkd. "Made in USA," 10" l $24

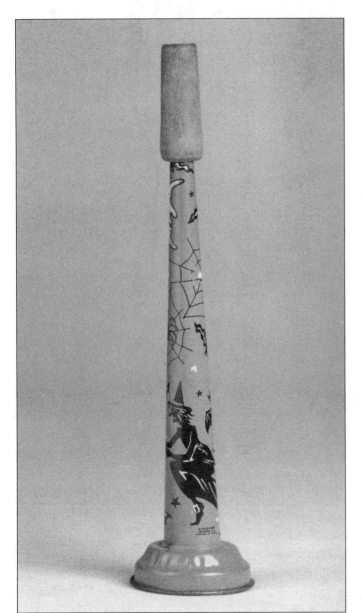

Napkin, mkd. "Made in USA," 8" sq. $5 ea.

Horn, tin and wood, orange and black, mkd. "Kirchnof, New-ark, NJ, Made in USA," 8" h $40

Clacker and horn, tin with wood mouth piece and paper jack-ó-lantern face, 9" l $45

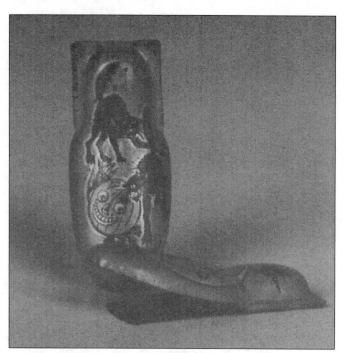

Noisemaker, lithographed paper and wood, paper rolls out when blown, 3" when rolled $28

Clickers, tin, mkd. "Kircho, Made in USA," 2" l $15ea.

Rattle, lithographed tin with wooden handle, orange black and yellow, mkd. "Kirchnof, Life Of The Party Products," 4" h $30

Noisemaker, wood with black composition cat, mkd. "Germany," 7-1/2" l $150

Rattle, lithographed tin with wood handle, orange, black and white, mkd. "Made in USA," 4" l $35

Clacker, lithographed tin with wood clapper, mkd. "J. Chein & Co., Made in USA," 9" l $42

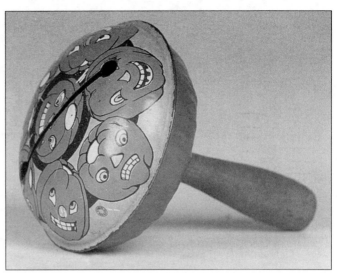

Rattle, lithographed tin with wood handle, orange, black and green, mkd. "T. Cohn, Inc., Made in USA," 5" l $35

Horn, wood, cardboard and crepe paper, orange and black, 7-1/2" l $45

Frog clicker, lithographed tin, orange and black, mkd. "T. Cohn, Inc., Made in USA," 3-1/4" l $28

Postcards, L- children bobbing for apples, Raphael Tuck & Sons, Hallowe'en Series No. 150, 1908 $12 , R- Witch dancing with vegetable man and cat, Raphael Tuck & Sons, Hallowe'en Series No. 150 $15

Postcards, L- Boy carving jack-o'-lantern, 1910 $10 , R- Witch reading cards, printed in Germany $15

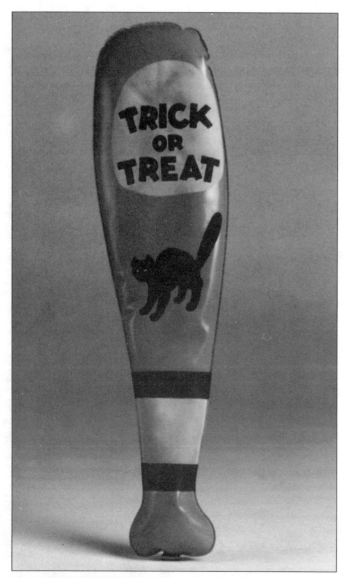

Toy, Inflated "ball" bat, orange yellow and black, plastic, mkd. "Alvimar Manuf. Co., Inc., NY," 10" l $6

Toy, "Flip-Flop Jack-o'-lantern," inflated plastic, "Alvimar Manuf. Co., Inc., NY," 5" h $8

Pair of mice, rabbit fur and pipe cleaner bodies, trimmed with red and pink felt, mkd. "Original Fur Toys Made in W. Germany," 2" h $38

Trio of valentine people, cotton batting heads, chenille body, crepe paper hats, 1930s, 6-1/2" h $75

Valentine couple, cotton batting heads, wire bodies covered in shirred crepe paper, 1920s, 12" h $90

Dimensional, two-sided, steam engine and tender, connected by red and pink honeycomb, Mkd. "Printed in Germany," 18" l $95

Calling cards $3 ea.

Dimensional, lithographed, embossed, Germany, 8-1/2" h $35

The Farmer's Wife Magazine, February 1938 $20

Potato, candy container, molded cardboard, cloth shamrock on top, 3-1/2" l $60

Top hat, candy container, top of hat opens, cardboard, mkd. "St. Patrick's Hat, Loft Candy Corp., Long Island City, NY," 2-1/2" h $50

Flat/three dimensional, cardboard leprechaun on tissue paper honeycomb toadstool, mkd. "Beistle Co., Made in USA," 13" h $12

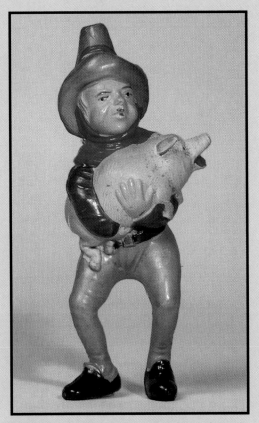

Irish man holding pig, celluloid, weighted base, mkd. "Japan," 6" h $75

Doll, composition, green and white flannel clothing, painted face, original box, mkd. "Japan," 4-1/4" h $65

Lapel pins, wire with green or white silk thread, bisque hats, 1-3/4" h, ea., $2

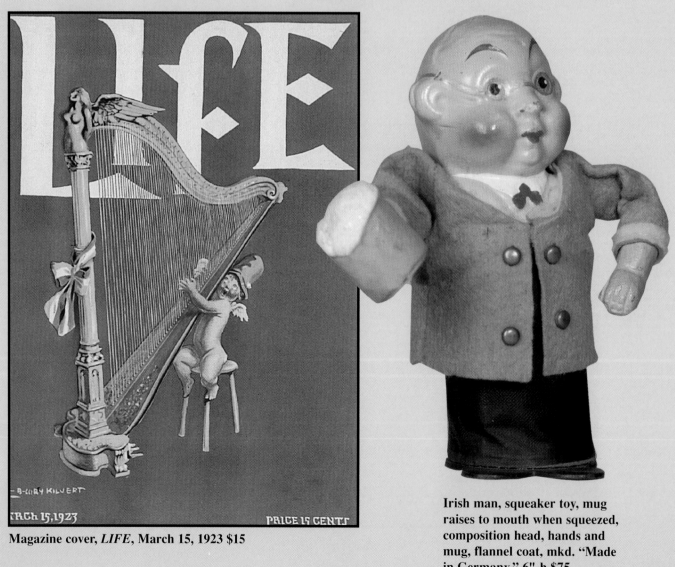

Magazine cover, *LIFE*, March 15, 1923 $15

Irish man, squeaker toy, mug raises to mouth when squeezed, composition head, hands and mug, flannel coat, mkd. "Made in Germany," 6" h $75

Basket and chicks candy container, one chick lifts up to reveal place for candy, chicks are composition, dried moss nest, mkd. "Germany," 5" d $65

Rabbit, papier-mâché candy container, opening in base, paper label eyes, 16" d $70

Basket with glass egg, egg has hand-painted scene dated "1897," basket has paper label on base mkd. "Germany" $95

Chicken candy container, molded cardboard, splits in middle of body, glass eyes, mkd. "West Germany," 7" h $38

Rabbit on tricycle, wind-up, metal tricycle with missing handlebars, celluloid rabbit, mkd. "Made in Japan," 3-1/2" l $15

Magazine cover, *LIFE*, Easter, 1904 $18

Rabbit head bank, hard plastic, mkd. "Round Tubes & Cores, Chicago, Illinois," 6-1/4" d $18

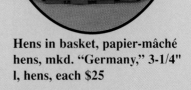

Hens in basket, papier-mâché hens, mkd. "Germany," 3-1/4" l, hens, each $25

Postcards, L-R, L: 1912, R: mkd. "Tuck Lincoln's Birthday Series No.155, Printed in Saxony" $5 ea.

Magazine cover, *Leslie's Weekly*, July 6, 1905 $18

Log candy container, cardboard with composition berries and satin ribbon, mkd. "Japan," 5" l $70

Postcard "Made in Germany, NN0586"

Postcard "M.W. Taggart, New York, copyright, 1908" $4 ea.

Flat decoration, cat, embossed cardboard, mkd.
"Made in USA, Copr. H.E. Luhrs," 18" h $95

Flat decoration, owl, embossed cardboard,
mkd. "79 cents," 22" h $25

Flat decoration, cat, cardboard, movable arms, legs and tail,
mkd. "Beistle Co., Made in USA," 6" h $18

Figure, witch on pumpkin, papier-mâché,
5-1/2" h $95

Mask, woman, papier-mâché, mkd. "Made in Germany," 7" h $35

Mask, duck, gauze, 7-1/2" h $40

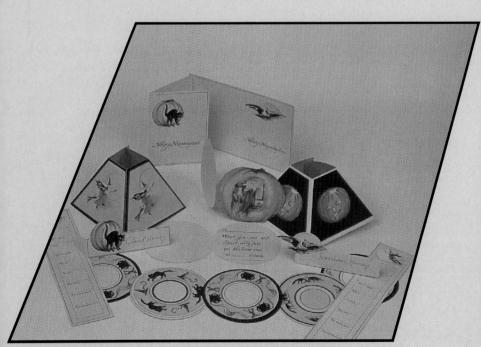

Peggy's Halloween Party Box sample contents, complete set has 52 pcs., Barse & Hopkin, Pub., NY $125

Noisemaker, wood with molded cardboard jack-o'-lantern head, mkd. "Germany," 8-1/2" l $250

Tambourine with witch head, lithographed tin, mkd. "T. Cohn, Inc., Brooklyn, NY," 7" d $60

Horn, turned wood, mkd. "Czecho-Slovakia," 4-1/2" h $40

Turkey, Celluloid, red, white, and blue 1930s, 4" h $15

Turkeys, hard plastic, USA, L-R, 1-3/4" h $12, 3-1/2" h $20

Roast turkey, candy container, opening in base, pressed paper, 4" l, Germany $55

Magazine, *Farmer's Wife*, November 1936, cover illus. by C. Twelvetrees $10

Composition turkeys, Germany, L-R, candy container, solid base with opening, 1910-1930, 5" h $38, candy container, metal legs, removable head, 5-1/2" h $50, solid base, 3" h $28

Gobbler with place card holder at the base of metal spring legs, 1920, 2-1/2" h $18

Magazine, *Woman's World*, November 1934, cover illus. by Miriam Story Hurford $5

Menu booklet & souvenir, Thanksgiving, November 28, 1935, Company "A" 66th Infantry (Light Tanks), Fort George G. Meade, Maryland, cover illus. of pilgrim toting a rifle and carrying a turkey $10

Toy, wind-up, cloth head and body, plastic eyes and legs, lithographed wings and tail, mkd. "Made in Japan," 6" h $75

Postcards, L-R, "Wishing You a Happy Thanksgiving," Germany, 1910, embossed silver background, turkey perched on an American flag $4; "Thanksgiving Greetings," turkey chasing a boy with a football, Germany, 1908 $5

Father Christmas quartet —L-R—Yellow, 9-3/4" h $850; Red, 14 -1/4" h $1000; White, 6" h $300; Blue, 9-3/4" h $1000

Scrapbook, brown leather cover with embossed Father Christmas figures and gold holly leaves, mkd. PAT. MARCH 1876, 11-1/2" h, $125

"Fairy Christmas Soap" display box, cloth covered with latch, 16"x16" $170

Christmas figures — trio of carolers, composition, flocked coats and hats, spring mounted heads, candy containers, 1930s, Germany, 6" h, $70

Noma Decorative
Light Set in original
box, lithographed box
with Santa, USA $10

Wax over composition angel, human hair wig, spun glass wings, cloth dress, Germany, 4" l, $55

Silvered glass ball, indent, 2-1/2" h $3

Paper cornucopia, with dresden
and chromo-lithograph trim,
gauze string, early 1900s,
USA/Germany, 9" h $70

Glass figural, gold teapot, Germany, 4" h $35

Gift tags, USA, each $1

German one-piece street scene, 4 houses and a church, early 1900s, marked Germany, 7"x 8" h, $30

Sheet music, "Santa Claus Is Comin' To Town," pub. Leo Feist $12

1912 calendar pennant, cardboard w. Santa postcard insert, Miller New York Racket Store, Lock Haven, PA, 17-1/2" l $25

Santa bank, chalkware, 1950s, 10" h $45

Cotton batting Santa, tomato soup red coat, composition face, black oil cloth belt, Japan, 7-1/2" h, 1920s, $48

Battery-operated Santa, metal, covered with red and white plush suit and hat, soft plastic face, holding metal wand with white star light, wand moves up and down while Santa's head turns, 10" h, $110

Set of 8 candy container houses, original box, lithographed cardboard w. mica trim, Japan, 1930s, $72

L-R, Japanese house, 3" h $8; German house, 3" h $15

CHAPTER 6

THANKSGIVING

Harvest Festivals have been a part of almost every culture throughout the history of man. From Egyptians to Syrians, from Romans to Jews, and the North American Indians, Thanksgiving was a holiday to give thanks for the harvest and still is an important yearly event today.

The Pilgrims of the Plymouth Colony, after surviving the deprivation of their first winter, set aside a time in the fall of 1621 to give thanks for their first harvest. This three-day event is credited as America's first Thanksgiving. Proclaiming a day of thanks was a tradition transplanted from Europe and frequently celebrated by English settlers to celebrate the safe crossing of the Atlantic.

Starvation was a constant threat to Plymouth Colony, so food was central to that first Thanksgiving. The invited Indians contributed deer, the men of the colony provided fowl, fish were plentiful, and the first corn harvest provided the staples for the meal. As a result, a feast became the most important activity in the American Thanksgiving.

For years following 1621, Thanksgiving "was" not a regular event. Proclaimed by the church and later by political leaders, days of thanksgiving were designated to celebrate successes in the Revolutionary War, and by Presidents George Washington, John Adams, and James Madison.

Thanksgiving days, by the middle of the19th century, were common but scheduled by individual states or even local governments. Credited to a campaign by Sarah Joseph Hale, editor of *Godey's Lady's Book*, President Lincoln set the last Thursday in November as a national day of thanksgiving. This date remained fixed until Franklin Delano Roosevelt changed the time to a week earlier to increase the length of the Christmas buying season and combat the Depression. This change caused such a debate, that in 1941, Congress set the fourth Thursday

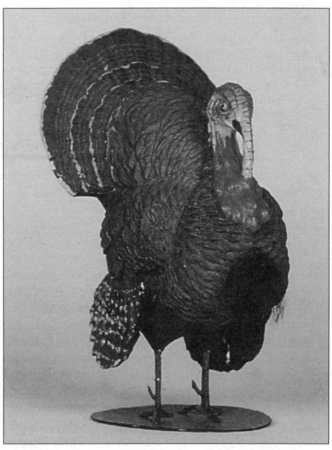

Turkey candy container, composition, metal legs, removable head, Germany, 8" $250

of November as the permanent date of our day of Thanksgiving.

The decorations for Thanksgiving almost all center on favors, place markers, and centerpieces for the feast table. In addition to turkeys, animals and people made of joined vegetables are listed in catalogs of the early 20th century. Many of these items now appear in books as Halloween items.

Book

Golden Harvest Days, Davis C. Cook Pub. Co., Elgin, Ill., 1910 . . . . $15
The Giant Thanksgiving Book, by Lenore Hetrick, Paine Publishing Co., Dayton, Ohio $18

Candy Container

Rooster, removable head, composition, metal feet, shades of brown, Germany, 5" h $75

Figures:

Miscellaneous

Human figure with vegetable head, celluloid, USA, 1920s, 3-1/2" h $60
Rooster, chicken, duck or goose, metal legs, Germany, composition, 1910-1930, 3" h $10
Rooster, celluloid, shades of gray with green, red and yellow highlights, 3-1/2" h $35

Pilgrims

Couple, molded pot metal, painted, 4" h $85
Couple, wax, 3" h. $5

Turkeys

Composition gobbler
   metal legs, Germany, 1910-1930, 3-1/2" h . . $30
   metal legs, Germany, 1910-1930, 2-1/2" h . . $25
   solid base, Germany, 1920, 4-1/2" h $35
   solid base, Germany, 1920, 3" h $28
   solid base, Japan, 1930s, 3-1/2" h. $22
   solid base, Japan, 1930s, 2" h. $20
   solid base, USA, 1930, 3"h $25
Composition gobbler candy container opening in
   back, metal legs, Germany, 1900-1910, 5" h. $45
Composition, hen metal legs, Germany, 1910-1930,
   2-1/2" h $30
Glass painted candy container, 8" h, USA. $75
Hard Plastic sitting gobbler, USA, 1950s, 2-1/2" h .$10
Pot, metal gobbler, standing, Britains Ltd., England,
   1" h. $25
Wax gobbler, USA, 4" h. $5

Miscellaneous

Peggy's Thanksgiving Party Box, 48 pcs., contains
   lamp shades, doilies, bon-bon dishes, place
   cards, invitations and trays $45
Platter, turkey in a pastoral scene, floral border, 23,"
   mkd. England. $300

Paper

Flat Decorations

Set, "4 Colorful Thanksgiving Cutouts," turkey gobbler, corn shock, maple leaf, pilgrim hunter, paper,
   mkd. "Made in USA," original glassine envelope,
   1940s, 12-1/2" h. $30
Turkey, cardboard, green, brown and red, 1930s, 3"
   h. $9

Pilgrim couple and Indian, cardboard with easel back, Denni-
son, USA, 1960s, 15-1/2" h $10 ea.

Pilgrim boy, head only, cardboard place card, 3" h $2

Turkey, embossed cardboard, black, white and red,
   mkd. "Made in USA," 9-1/2" h $20

Magazines

Good Housekeeping, November, 1945, little girl
   holding silverware waiting for dinner on cover $12
Home Arts, November, 1930, woman sewing stuff-
   ing in turkey on cover $8
Life, Thanksgiving, 1904, woman holding pumpkin
   surrounded by scenes of the turkey before and after on cover $15
People's Popular Magazine, November 1918, two
   children carrying a harvest basket on cover, illus.
   by Anna Ames Howes $15

Pilgrims

Couple, cardboard with blue honeycomb fold-out
   body and feet, mkd. "Made in USA, Beistle Co.,"
   13-1/2" h $30

Postcards

"May glad Thanksgiving crown your days and
   years," young woman cradling turkey in her arms,
   International Art Pub. Co., printed in Germany,
   1912. . . . . $4
"Thanksgiving Greetings," boy and girl with two tur-
   keys, 1909 . . . . $4
"Thanksgiving Greetings," pair of turkeys, printed in
   Germany $4
"Thanksgiving Greetings," three white turkeys in
   pastoral scene, 1912. . . . . $3
"Thanksgiving Greetings," turkey on a throne with
   patriotic symbols, 1909 . . . . $4

Composition turkeys, USA, L-R, 5" h $45, 4" h with metal legs $40, 3-1/2" h $35

Candy container pair of turkeys, composition, Germany, 1910-1930, hen, removable head, metal legs, 5" h $90, gobbler, removable head, metal legs, horsehair beard, 5" h $60

Gobbler, with folded tail, molded, Japan, 1930s, 6" h $40

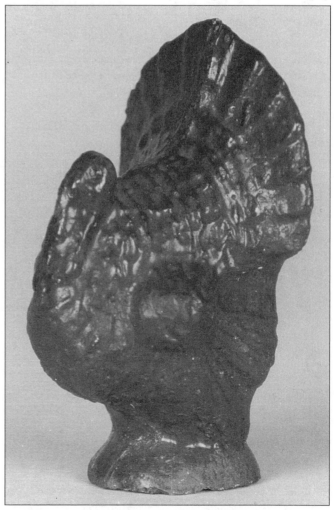

Plaster gobbler, molded, brown, homemade, USA, 1950s, 4-1/2" h $12

Turkeys, L-R, hard rubber, no legs, 2-1/2" h $10, pair of pot metal, 1" h $45

Pressed cardboard candy container, opening in base, orange/tan, mkd. "ATCO Co.," USA, 7" h $65

Composition, table set, one centerpiece gobbler 4-3/4" h and one place card turkeys, metal legs on cardboard base, Germany, 3" h $70

Booklet, "Choice Thanksgiving Entertainments," Paine Publishing Co., Dayton, Ohio $12

Greeting cards, created with watercolor and pieces of postage stamps, L-R, "Greetings For A Joyous Thanksgiving," picture of boy hiding hatchet behind back and turkey, "The Mayflower – With Joyful Thanksgiving Wishes," Mayflower near the coast $8 ea.

Turkeys, cardboard, L-R, "Turkey Gobbler Centerpiece," USA, color printed each side, honeycomb tissue paper base, 9" h, 1940s $15; cardboard, double-sided, lithographed, 11" h, stand-up display, attached wings, Dennison, USA, 1950s $22

Cardboard, L-R, lithographed, Germany, easel base, 4" h $18; easel back, mkd. "Made in USA," 1960s, 7" h $8; heavily embossed turkey, sepia tones, easel back, 5" h, 1910 $12

Box, tin, pilgrims landing in America pictured on hinged lid, Nabisco, USA, 8-1/2"x11"x3" $35

 **CHAPTER 7**

CHRISTMAS

Christmas, the most popular of the annual holidays, is celebrated during the winter solstice. Most cultures throughout history have marked this time of the sun's rebirth and the beginning of the gradual increase of daylight hours. Even before the birth of Christ, the winter solstice was celebrated as the anniversary of several ancient gods' births. While it is impossible to determine the exact date when Christ was born, by the year 356, December 25 was accepted.

As the celebration of Christ's birth and Christianity increased in popularity, pagan practices declined. However, there were some pagan practices that became absorbed with Christian traditions. The Romans introduced the traditions of decorating with flowers and candles and the giving of gifts. The Celtic cultures added draping the home with evergreens, mistletoe and holly.

Many more prominent Christmas traditions appeared in the Middle Ages. For example, during the fourteenth century, the religious celebration of Christ's birth involved the use of Christmas carols, and in Italy, the live re-enactment of the Nativity. The re-enactment evolved into the tradition of modeling Christ's birth with figures created from various materials.

Churches in eighteenth century Germany used a Christmas pyramid to display scenes of Christ's birth. This pyramid or set of shelves was often decorated with evergreen branches and some people believe that this pyramid was a forerunner of the Christmas tree. The displays eventually outgrew the pyramid and entire corners and altars in churches were utilized for the elaborate nativities.

People re-created these scenes in their homes and this tradition was carried to America by the Moravian sect. Their putz, meaning, "to decorate," filled entire rooms. This practice was generally accepted and crèche or putz scenes were commonly found in homes by the century's turn. With the growing popularity of the Christmas tree, the putz displays were a perfect way to fill the space at the tree's base.

By the 1500s in Europe, the evergreen tree was an important part of the Christmas tradition. With the assistance of Martin Luther and Queen Victoria the evergreen tree as a Christmas tradition spread throughout the world. Early Christmas trees were decorated with fruit, cookies, small gifts and homemade fancies. Since the late 1800s, artificial trees have been made with materials ranging from goose feathers to aluminum.

Santa Matches, "Lion Match Co.," 4" h, $10

The Christian St. Nicholas combined with traits from the Scandinavian Thor, the Anglo-Saxon Father Christmas, and the Russian Kolwada and Babouska evolved into the Dutch Sinterklaas. Sinterklaas emigrated to America with the Dutch settlement of New York. Thanks to Washington Irving, Thomas Nast and Haddon Sundblum of the Coca-Cola Company, Sinterklaas became our Santa Claus.

ADVERTISING

Bank Deposit Book
For Christmas Club, gold cover with Santa looking in the window, 1935, 5" h $8

Books
The Night Before Christmas, Bush and Bull Co. Dept. Store, Williamsport, PA, 12-3/4" h $25

Santa Claus Book, L.L. Stearns and Sons, Williamsport, PA, published by Charles E. Graham & Co., Newark, NJ, 9-1/2" h $15

101 Meat Recipes Old and New, Holiday Greeting, Lundy's Meat Market, Broad St., Montoursville, PA, 1927, 8" h $5

Santa's Greeting, Pomeroy's, The Harter Publishing Co., 1932, 11" h. $10

Pin, "Merry Christmas Butler Bros. Co.," Santa head pictured, Baltimore Badge & Novelty Co., Baltimore, MD, 1-1/4" d $8
Pin, "Shop in Pottsville," Santa head pictured, Philadelphia Badge Co., 1-1/4" d $10

Booklets

"Christmas Carol by Charles Dickens," L.L. Stearn's and Sons, 100pgs., 5" h $7
"Christmas Carols," 1st National Bank of Danville, PA, copyright 1949, Christmas Club A Corp, NY, NY, three children singing pictured on front, 6" h . . . $5
Samples printed menu card, "Christmas Greetings," Lenox Manufacturing Co., Plainfield, NJ, 1909, 8"x6" $9
"The Night Before Christmas," A.B. Wyckoff-Sears Store, Stroudsburg, PA, Newton, NJ, Hackettstown, NJ, Whitman Pub. Co., 1937, 6" h . . $6
"When All The World Is Kin," Christmas giveaway for Fowler, Dick, and Walker Boston Store, Wilkes-Barre, 1920, 5" h $7

Box

Tin, Nabisco, Christmas visitor pictured on the hinged lid, 8-1/2"x11"x3" $25

Calendar

Celluloid, Christmas Giveaway, The Penny Specialty Shop, Selinsgrove, PA, framed winter scene with holly and two birds, 1929, 7-3/4"x3" $12

Candy tins

2 lb., Mrs. Steven's Co., red with Santa Claus on cover, 8-1/2" d $10
With handle, "Satin Finish, Madison Mixed Hard Candies," Ludens Inc., Reading, PA, 2-1/4"x9" . . . $15
Santa face lithographed on cover, surrounded by holly leaves, 4" diameter $70

Cards

Gift subscription notification, *Farm Journal*, winter scene, 1940s, 4" h $4
Giveaway, Christmas Club, cut-out Santa holding a helicopter, Hamburg Savings Bank, New York, NY, 6" h $7
Giveaway, Christmas Club, cut-out Santa holding a slate, Robesonia State Bank, 1929, 6-1/2" h. $10

Giveaway, Dundee Smart Clothes, Allentown, PA, cut-out Santa, 1941, 6" h $8
War bond certificate, "So There'll Always Be a Christmas, My War Bond Gift to You," 1943, 5"x9" . . .$8

Coin Holder

Stocking shaped, "1st National Bank of Milton, Milton, Pa.," 6" h $5

Matchbook

Boehmer's Garage, Milton, PA, printed by Giant Feature Matchbook, Lyon Match Co., NY, blue cover with winter scene, matchsticks look like candles, 4-1/4" h $10

Pin

Celluloid on straight pin, "Gifts For Everybody," cut-out Santa figure, C.K. Whitner & Co., Reading, PA, 1-1/2" h $15

Pinback button, celluloid on tin

"Meet Me At Kline, Eppehimer, & Co.," Keystone Badge Co., Reading, PA, 3/4" d $8

Pinback buttons, metal

"Health For All," Santa head pictured, National Tuberculosis Association, 3/4" d $7
"Health To All," Santa head pictured, National Tuberculosis Assoc., 3/4" d $7
"Santa's Visitor North Pole, New York," Santa, reindeer and North Pole pictured, 1960s, 1-1/2" d $7
"Visit Our Toyland at Guinan's," Santa head pictured, 1-1/4" d $5

Plate

China, "Souvenir of Sunbury, PA," white with gold trim, Santa and sleigh with holly in center, 6-1/2" d. . $20

Trade Cards

"Ehrich's Trade Goods," printed by Burrow-Giles Lith. Co., 20 & 22 Gold St., New York, when folded sleep-

Trade Card, "Woolson Spice Cos., Holiday Greeting," 1892, 5"x7" $10

ing girl titled "The Child's Dream," when open Father Christmas with toys pictured, 1882, 4" h $10

"Santa Claus Soap, Gifts for Wrappers," N. K. Fairbanks Co., Chicago, St. Louis, New York, Santa carrying a soap box, 1899, 3"x 5" $10

"THE WHITE is King of all Sewing Machines, 80,000 now in use," child holding snowballs, mkd. on back "J. Saltzer, Pianos, Organs & Sewing Machines, Bloomsburg, Pa." $10

BOOKS

Around The World With Santa Claus, McLoughlin Bros., New York, 1900, 12" h $30

The Night Before Christmas, Eileen Fox Vaughan, Whitman Pub. Co., 1949, 12" h $15

Night Before Christmas - Linenette, Sam'l Gabriel Sons & Co., New York, 1947, 12" h $25

Night Before Christmas or A Visit of St. Nicholas, McLoughlin Bros., New York, 1896, 12" h . . . $30

Santa Claus Comes To America, written and illus. by Caroline Singer and Cyrus Leroy Baldridge, Alfred A. Knopf, New York, 1942 . . . . $30

Santa Claus In StoryLand, pop-up book, Doehla Greeting Cards Inc., Fitchburg, Mass., 1950, 11" h. . .$25

Santa Claus Stories #0461 Santa Claus Series, Graham & Matlack, New York, 9-1/2" h $20

The Night Before Christmas - A Golden Book, Golden Press, Western Pub. Co., Racine, Wisconsin, 1975, 15" $10

The Night Before Christmas, illus. by Francis B. Brundage, Saalfield Pub. Co., Akron, Ohio, 15" h $30

The Night Before Christmas, Merrill Pub. Co., 1937, 12-1/2" h $20

Watching For Santa Claus, Hurst & Co. Pub., New York, 1912, 9-1/2" h. $15

When Polly Ann Played Santa Claus by Eleanor H. Porter, Evergreen Series, Houghton Mifflin Co., Boston, New York, 1923, 6-1/2" h $10

Store display, "And Best of All, A Philco, Litho Co., USA,"
10"x9-1/2" $20

Feather trees, L-R, white, Germany, 10-1/2" h $85; green, Germany, 12" h $100

CHRISTMAS FIGURES

Angel

Wax, cardboard base, white with yellow hair, 3-1/2" h $3

Wax, cardboard base, white with yellow hair, Gurley Novelty Co., Buffalo, NY, copyright 1950, 4-3/4" $5

Boot

Hard plastic, red with cardboard band around top, originally filled with candy, "E. Rosen Co., Providence, RI, 4" h. $5

Molded cardboard, white with mica, "Kentucky Tavern" molded on side, 9" h $30

papier-mâché, red

    4" h $12
    5" h $15
    6" h $20
    7"x7" $25
    18" h $50

Choir Boys/Carolers

Choir boy, hard plastic, red and white, 3-1/2" h. . $4

Choir boy, wax candle, black and white, USA, 3" h $3

Elf

Bisque, elves came in a variety of colors and positions, mkd. "Japan" on base, 2-1/2" to 3" h, each $15

China, green suit, reclining position, foil paper label "Japan," 2-1/2" h $4

Book, The Manger Babe, *1916 Stecher Litho Co., Rochester, NY, illus. by Margaret Evans Price, verses by Isabelle C. Byrum, 13-3/4"x7-1/2" $20*

Pinecone body, cardboard base, cotton batting head, holding pipe cleaner candy cane, Japan, 3" h. $8
Pinecone body, cardboard base, cotton batting head, composition face, holding composition red and white mushroom, Japan, 3" h $10

LIGHTS and LIGHT BULBS

Lights:

Candle

One, hard plastic, white, 5"x9" h $3
Three in one base, hard plastic, white, 9" h. $6
Five in one base, hard plastic, white, 14" x9" h . $10
One, metal base, green with enameled, embossed designs, green and red cardboard tube, made in USA, 3-1/2"x9" h $10
One, metal base, spatter painted red on green, red and silver cardboard tube, 3-1/2"x9" h. $10

Light Accessories:

Shades

"Popeye-Cheers," multicolored, plastic, Royal Electric Co., Pawtucket, RI, set of eight $50
"Whirl-Glo," multicolored, paper, Sail-Me Co., Chicago, set of six $20

Light bulbs

Bubblelights, set, working order, 1950s $6
Angel, red lacquered milk glass, 3" h $20
Bell, embossed Santa face, lacquered milk glass, red, green and white, 2-3/4" h $15
Cat holding ball, lacquered milk glass, multicolored, 3" h $75
Dick Tracy, lacquered milk glass, full figure, 1940s $65
Father Christmas, lacquered clear glass, multicolored, European, pre-1920, 6" h $85
Grapes, lacquered milk glass, red and white, 3" h $20
House, lacquered milk glass, red and green, 2-1/2" h $20
Indian, lacquered clear glass, full figure, multicolored, European, 3-3/4" h $300
Japanese lantern, cylinder, lacquered milk glass, multicolored, 5" $20

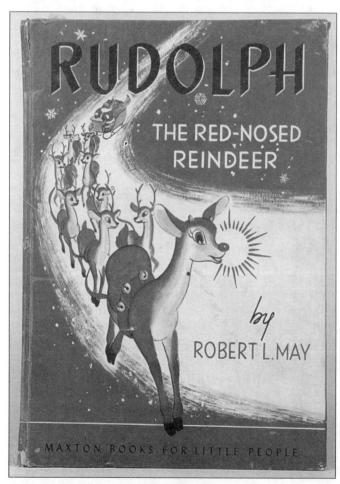

Book, Rudolph The Red-Nosed Reindeer *by Robert L. May, Maxton publishers Inc., New York, NY, 1939 $15*

Japanese lantern, oval, lacquered milk glass, multi-
colored, 2" h. $10
Parrot, lacquered milk glass, multicolored, 3-1/2" h $25
Pear, lacquered clear glass, multicolored, Europe-
an, 2-1/2" h $20
Santa, full figure, holding pack, lacquered milk glass,
red and black, 3-1/2" h. $25
Santa head, lacquered milk glass, red and white
2-1/2" h $20
Songbird, lacquered milk glass, blue, 3" h. $15
Snowman, lacquered clear glass, white with red hat,
European, pre 1920, 3" h. $20

NATIVITY

Animals, celluloid

Camel, brown, mkd. "USA," 1-1/2" h $6
Camel, red, mkd. "Japan," 3" h $10
Cow, lying down, brown, mkd. "Irwin," 3-1/2" h . . $8
Cow, standing, purple, 2-1/2" h $8
Donkey, black and white, nodder, 3" h $15
Donkey, white, black and brown, 3" h $10
Elephant, gray, mkd. "Japan," 3" h $12
Goat, beige and black, 2-1/4" h $10
Goat, white, 2-1/2" h $10
Horse, black and white, 3" h $8
Sheep, black and white, Japan, 2" h $10

Book, Christmas Blossoms, *Holly Leaf Series, 1899, McLoughlin Bros., NY, 8"x9 -1/4" $20*

Santa's Surprise Paint Book, *Merrill Co., 1949, 15" h $12*

Animals, composition, Germany

Camel, brown, lying down, flocked, 3" h $35
Camel, brown, standing, string halter, wooden legs,
5-1/2" h $40
Cow, brown, standing, wooden legs, 4" h $30
Bull, flannel covered, metal horns, brown and white,
wooden legs, 3-1/2" h $30
Bull, wooden legs, wood horns, flocked, brown,
4-1/2" h $35
Calf, wooden legs, black and white, 2" h $20
Donkey, gray, wooden legs, 3-1/2" h $30
Elephant, gray, flocked, bone tusks, cloth on back,
4-1/2" h $60
Elephant, gray, painted tusks, 4" h $50
Goat, flannel covered, white, paper collar, wooden
legs, metal horns, 2" h. $30
wooden horns, 3-1/2" h $35
Goat, flannel covered, brown and white spots, paper
collar with bell, metal horns, 3-1/2" h $40
Horse
black and brown, 4" h $30
brown, wooden legs, 4" h $35
Sheep, composition base, white flocked, 2-1/2" h $25

Stocking, red felt with white litho, 14" l $15

Sheep, white, wooden legs, 2" h $25
Sheep, flannel covered, paper collar with bell, wood-
    en legs, black, 3" h. $40
    white, 3" h $35
    white, 4" h $45
Sheep, wool covered, paper collar, wooden legs,
    white,
    3-1/2" h $40
    4-1/2" h $50
Animals, plaster, Japan
    camel, standing, brown with red blanket, 4" h $10
    cow, lying in grass, mkd. "Japan," 3" h $8
    donkey, standing in grass, gray, mkd. "Japan,"
      3-1/2" h $8
    sheep, standing in grass, white, mkd. "Japan,"
      1-1/2" h $5

Nativity Figures:

Angel
    bisque, white and gold, Japan, 3" h $7
    composition, kneeling, white robe, gold wings,
      Germany, 5-1/2" h. $25
    hard plastic, white and gold, USA, 4" h $4
Attendant
    Moor, red fez, hand raised to hold camel halter,
      composition, Germany, 5-1/2" h $30

Baby Jesus
    composition crib 3"x2" h, molded wax baby, 1-1/2"
      l, Germany $30
    molded plaster Baby and crib, Japan, 2" h . . . $5
    goose girl, European dress, holding stick and
      chicken, composition, painted flowers on base,
      Germany, 5-1/2" h $35
Joseph
    kneeling, bisque, Japan, 4" h $7
    kneeling, composition, Germany, 5-1/2" h. . . $20
    kneeling, plaster, Japan, 3" h $5
Mary
    kneeling, composition, Germany, 5-1/2" h. . . $20
    kneeling, hard plastic, USA, 3" h. $4
    kneeling, plaster, Japan, 3" h $5
Palm tree, painted composition base, brown trunk
    covered with cut paper, green branches covered
    with cut paper, Germany, 7" h. $30
Shepherd
    bisque, standing, Japan, 4-1/2" h $7
    hard plastic, standing, 5" h $4
    plaster, kneeling, holding sheep, 3" h $6
Shepherd, composition, Germany
    European dress, holding hat, 6" h $25
    Mid-Eastern dress, kneeling, 4" h $20
    Mid-Eastern dress, elderly, holding shepherd's
      crook, 6" h. $20
Wise Men/Kings
    bisque, kneeling, holding gift, 3" h $6
    plaster, standing, holding gift, 5" h $4
Wise Men/Kings, composition, Germany
    holding gift, standing, 6-1/2" h. $20

Record, 78 rpm, "O Little Town of Bethlehem," Record Guild of America Inc., NY $5

Nativity Sets:

Cardboard
boxed set, 1950s, USA $20

Paper, fold-out
fold-out, 4" h, mkd. "Germany" $20

ORNAMENTS

Cardboard
Ball, two piece, covered with lithographed scenes of children, mkd. "West Germany" inside the ball, string hanger, 4" h $15
Ball, two-piece, lithographed "Man in the Moon," Germany, 4" h $150
Church, pointed steeple, white, mica covered, mkd. "Czechoslovakian," 3" h. $12
Church, onion dome, multicolored, mkd. "Czecho-slovakian," 3" h $12
House, multicolored with black-silver mica, mkd. " Japan," 2" h $10
House, white, mica covered, mkd. "Czechoslovaki-an," 2" h. $10

Celluloid
Ball, blue, celluloid hanger, 3" d $7
Ball, multicolored, celluloid hanger, 4" d $10
Bird on a ring, yellow bird and green ring, mkd. " Japan" on a paper label, 6" h. $40
Santa Claus, red with white, standing, celluloid hanger, Irwin Co., USA, 4" h $45

Chromolithograph
Angel, head surrounded by green gauze, paper lace skirt, gold foil trim, Germany, 7-1/2" h $20
Angel, surrounded by spun glass, Germany, 2-1/2" h $12

Fireplace, red and white with silver foil stocking, red chenille trim, wood sticks in firebox with metal fender, Japan, 3-1/4" h $18

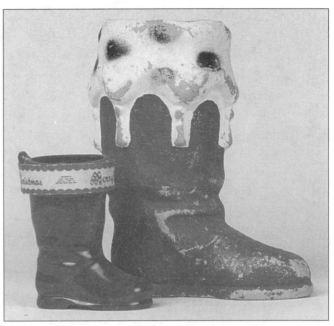

Boots, L-R, red plastic with cardboard label mkd. "Merry Christmas," Rosbro Plastics, Providence, RI, 4" h $5; red with white cuff, pressed cardboard, Atco Co., USA, 7-1/2" h $28

Angel, tree top ornament, dresden gold wings and star, spun glass halo, curled angel hair in center, mounted on cardboard tube, 9" h $45
Bell, blue, girl inside holding greens, tinsel trim, Germany, 5-1/2" h $8
Couple, winter dress, tinsel trim, Germany, 7-1/2" h $25
Girl, crepe paper skirt, tinsel background, Germany, 5" h $20
Girl, sleeping inside heart, surrounded by tinsel, Germany, 5" h $15
Santa and girl with toys, surrounded by tinsel, Germany, 8" h $25
Santa Claus, blue suit, Germany, 5" h $20
Santa Claus, cotton batting skirt with red crepe paper trim, Germany, 20" h $295
Santa Claus, pale red suit, holding tree, surrounded by blue flowers, tinsel trim, diamond shape, Germany, 11" h $35
Santa Claus, red suit, one foot in chimney, tinsel trim, Germany, 6-1/2" $30
Santa Claus, yellow suit, spun glass skirt, holding tree and toys, Germany, 9-1/2" h $30
Star, four angel heads inside, tinsel trim, Germany, 6" h $25

Cotton Batting
Apple, red and yellow, 1" h $8
Carrot, orange, 3" h. $10
Cigar, brown, 1" h $15
Girl, chromolithograph face, white cotton hood and coat, 4" h. $75
Lighthouse, white, red and black, 3" h. $25
Medicine bottle, white, 1-1/2" h $15

Hard plastic figures, red and white choir boy, 3-1/2" h, white and silver angel, 4" h $4 ea.

Pear, cloth leaf, yellow and orange, 3-1/2" $15
Santa Claus, composition face, white coat, standing
    in tinsel trim, 2" h $25
Turnip, red, blue and white, 3-1/2" h $20
Worm, green, 1-1/2" h $15

Dresdens, Flat, Germany
Reindeer, gold, red, and green foil, 7" w $65
Rooster, multicolored foil, 7" h $70
Star, embossed gold, tinsel trim, 3" h $30
Washtub, gold with chromolithograph baby in tub,
    5" w $70

Dresdens, 3-Dimensional, Germany
Alligator, silver, 4" l $190
Camel, brown, 3" h $140
Dirigible, silver, 6" l $240
Dog, beige and gray, 3" h $250
Fish, gold, 6" l $110
Fox, brown, 2" h. $160
Jockey on horse, brown, red and gray, 4" h . . $200
Mandolin, black and brown, 4". $110
Owl on branch, brown, black and white, 3" h. . $230
Reindeer, brown, 3" h $160
Reindeer pulling chariot, gold and red, 6" l . . . $140
Peacock, tail fanned, silver, blue and green, 6" h.$160
Slipper, blue, gauze top, 3" h. $170
Stork, black, white and red, 4" h $200
Turkey, iridescent reds and greens, tail fanned,
    4" h. $190
Turtle, green, 6" l $210

Glass, Ball
Green, unsilvered, 6" h $15
Gold and red with white stencil highlights, USSR
    Zone Germany mkd. cap, 1-3/4" h. $4

Pink, unsilvered, paper cap with string hanger, USA,
    4" h $4
Red, Shiny Brite, 3" h, USA, box of 6 . . . . $12
Red with frosted stencil picture of church, "Silent
    Night," Shiny Brite, USA, 3" h $2
Unsilvered, red and green painted stripes, metal
    cap, USA, 3" h. $3
Unsilvered, red, painted stripes, tinsel inside, USA,
    4" h $2
White with red stripes and silver glitter stars, plastic
    cap, West Germany, 2-1/2" h $2

Glass, Beaded
Cross, silver and red, two-dimensional, Japan, 4" h $25
Star, silver, two-dimensional, Czechoslovakia, 3" h . $20

Glass, Beads
Multicolored 1" beads of various shapes, paper label
    mkd. Germany, 36" l $40
Red 3/8" round balls, paper label mkd. "Japan,"
    48" l. $15
Red, white and blue-1/2" round balls, cardboard
    squares at each end, Germany, 10" l $10

Glass, Elliptical
White and pink, butterfly stencil, "Poland" mkd. on
    cap, 4" h $5
Unsilvered, red and blue painted stripes, tinsel in-
    side, USA, 4" h $3

Glass, Indent
Black with white painted highlights around the in-
    dent, 2" h. $3
Red, round with pointed base, "USA" mkd. on cap,
    3" h $3
Silver, red and blue, pointed base, "Shiny Brite" mkd.
    on cap, USA, 3" h $3

Glass, Figurals
Angel, red, Germany, 3-1/2" h. $75
Baby, in silver bag with red ribbon, Germany, 3" h $70
Bear, red, paws in muff, Germany, 4" h $75
Beehive, blue with painted gold bee, 3" h $40
Beetle, red on gold flower, 2-1/4" d $30

Bisque elves in various poses with Santa Claus, 1930s, mkd. Japan, elves $15, Santa $35

Bell, blue, unsilvered, paper cap and hanger, USA, 2-1/2" h $10

Birds

cockatoo, multicolored, spun glass tail, metal clip, Germany, 7" h $38

mallard, blue head, spun glass wings, annealed hook, 5" h $35

owl, red, black eyes and beak, Germany, 3" h $30

peacock, green with gold highlights, blue spun glass tail, clip, 4" h $25

songbirds, silver red and black, pair on one clip, Germany, 2-1/2" h $40

stork, silver and blue, spun glass tail, Germany, clip, 4" h $30

swan, silver with annealed hook, 3" h $35

swan, unsilvered, opaque pink, tinsel tail, lametta, Germany, 9-1/2" h $75

Bird cage, gold with painted bird, Germany, 2" h $30

Bird cage, pink, with white painted trim, Germany, 3-3/4" h $40

Bird in nest, unsilvered, 3 white frosted birds in red nest 2-1/4" h $70

Bugle, gold, Germany, 3 -1/4" l $25

Candy cane, silver with blue stripes, 6-1/2" l . . . $40

Car, red with tinsel hanger attached to each end of car, Germany, 3" h $100

Carousel, silver with red trim, Germany, 2-1/2" h. $65

Carrot, orange, green tucksheer leaf, Germany, 3" l $60

Cat face, molded on long handled rattle, silver and gray, Germany, 4-3/4" h $90

Chandelier, silver with 3 white candles, Germany, 3" h $40

Child, red pajamas, mica hood, Germany, 4" h . $60

Church, red and pink, Germany, 3-1/2" h $40

Clock, cuckoo, paper face, Germany, 3-1/2" h . $55

Light and lighting Light bulbs, monkey, clown, Santa and cat, glass, Germany, 3" h, set of 4 $155

Clown, head, multicolored, Germany, 2 -1/4" h. $60

Clown on comet, multicolored, Germany, 3-1/2" h $125

Clown, standing, green, "My Darling" on front of costume, Germany, 4" h $45

Coin, gold, stag on face, Germany, 2" d $25

Corn, ear, silver with green husk, Germany, 3-1/2" l $50

Cucumber, silver and green, 4-1/2" l $45

Devil, head, silver/white skin with red and black highlights, Germany, 4" h $110

Dog in bag, blue and red, "My Darling" on bag, Germany, 3" h $80

Dog, pink collar, Germany, 3" h $50

Dog, Scotty, gold, Germany, 3-3/4" h $60

Doll head, girl with glass eyes, Germany, 2-1/2" h $95

Elephant, gold, parade dress, Germany, 3" h . . $80

Fish, gold and red, Germany, 3" l $35

Fish, green and silver, Germany, 6" l $70

Flower, gold, Germany, 2" h $15

Flower, white mica, unsilvered, paper leaves, clip, Germany, 3-1/2" h $30

Frog, silver and gold, Germany 3-3/4" l $65

Fruit basket, clear glass openwork basket, contains small glass colored fruit, Germany, 2-1/2" h . $45

Girl's face in flower, gold, Germany, 3" $90

Girl standing in flower, gold, clip, Germany, 4" h $70

Grapes, bunch, purple with green leaves, Germany, 4" h $55

Heart, gold, Germany, 2" h $15

House, blue with multicolored detail, Germany, 3" h $25

House, multicolored with molded turkey, Germany, 3" h $45

Hot air balloon, pink, scrap child riding, lametta ropes, Germany, 5" h $40

Icicle, silver with white mica snow on top, 6" h . $30

Keg, unsilvered, gold painted highlights, lametta trim, Germany, 2" l $65

"Keystone Cop," blue, Germany, 4" $150

Blown glass figures, L-R, silver and white penguin, 7" h $60; silver deer, 5-1/4" h $55

Japanese light bulbs, Santa, 4" h $35, Fish, 2-3/4" h $25, Lantern, 1-3/4" h $20

Lamp, silver with red shade, gold paper trim, Germany, 3" h. $35
Mandolin, red, Germany, 3" l. $35
Monkey, red, holding stick, Germany, 3" h $55
Mushroom, red cap with white dots, silver stem, Germany, 3" h $35
Parasol, gold, unsilvered, lametta wire trim, Germany, 11" h. $70
Parasol, pink with gold stripes, Germany, 12" h $50
Pinecone, silvered, 4" h. $20
Pipe, gold with molded and painted Queen's face on the bowl, Germany, 5" l $125
Pear, gold, molded face on one side, Germany, 2-3/4" h $85
Pocketwatch, green with paper face, Germany, 2" d$45
Santa Claus, gold long coat, Germany, 3-1/2" h $30
Santa Claus in chimney, red coat, Germany, 3-1/2" h $50
Santa Claus in gold stocking, Germany, 3-1/2" h. .$65
Santa Claus, red coat, painted face, "roly poly," Germany, 4" h $50
Santa Claus, red long coat, Germany, 4" h $30
Shell, blue, Germany, 2" h. $15
Ship, blue glass with gold dresden sails, lameta lines, Germany, 4-1/2" h $40
Snowman, unsilvered, white mica coating, Germany, 3-1/2" h. $30
Squirrel, red, sitting, holding nut, Germany, 2-1/4" h $50
Sugar bowl, gold with painted flowers, Germany, 2" h. $30
Teapot, silver with painted flowers, Germany, 2" h $30
Tree, evergreen, red with white painted snow, unsilvered, clip, Germany, 4" h $45
Tree, evergreen, red with elf and toadstools, unsilvered, clip, Germany, 4" h $65
Wine bottle, red, paper label "Malaga," Germany, 4" h. $50

Glass, Kugels

Ball, green, stamped brass cap, 2" d. $35
Ball, silver, stamped brass cap, 6" d $120
Grapes, blue, stamped brass cap, 4" h. $200
Pear, gold, stamped brass cap, 3" h $260

Hard Plastic

Ball, faceted silver, 2" h. $2
Bell, green hard plastic with hard plastic holly leaf and berry, USA, 2" h, set of six $6
Carousel with metal propeller in center, "Tinkle Toy Co.," Youngstown, Ohio, original box, 4-pak $15
Icicles, white plastic, "glow in the dark," plastic annealed hook, 4" l, set of 15 . . . . $3
Rudolph, brown and white, USA $5
Star, red, flat, five points, USA $1
Santa Claus, blue suit, USA $5
Santa Claus, red with rabbit fur trim, elastic string with bell hanger, 4-1/2" h. $12

Metal

Ball, tin, litho Santa, cloth hanger, mkd. England, 1-1/2" h $5
Basket, gold woven tin, 3" h $15
Basket, wire frame wrapped in lametta, metal leg base, 5" h $35
Bird cage, heavy tin, red lacquer, flat metal bird on swing, 4" h. $45
Elliptical, lacquered red and gold faceted indents, 4-1/2" h $15
Icicles, lead, silver, box with Santa trimming tree on cover, "Icicles," Metal Goods Corp., St. Louis, USA, box 9-3/4" h $10
Icicles, twisted, two-color (red/silver, blue/silver), 5" h, set of six $15
Reflector, star shaped, punched tin, 3" h $3
Star, eight point, soft metal, silver with red lacquered indents, 3-1/2" h $10

Glass beads, L-R, short set, Germany $25, long set, small beads, Japan $8

Miscellaneous:

China, Bell
  Girl in winter dress, brown hair, tinsel hanger,
    mkd. "Japan," 2" h. $12
  Santa, bust, blue pack over shoulder, mkd. "Ja-
    pan," 1-1/2" h, set of six $30
  Cornucopia, gold embossed dresden paper with
    scrap picture, cloth tape handle, 7" h $55
  Papier-mâché, boy, metal hanger in head, mkd.
    "Germany" on base, 6" h. $85
  Wax angel, white and yellow, metal hanger, 3" h.$4
  Santa Claus, red and white, metal hanger, 3" h$5
  Wreath, green, bottle brush, white mica, silver
    balls, red ribbon hanger, Japan, 3" h $8
  Wreath, red cellophane, green ribbon, 3" $4

PAPER

Calling Card

"A Merry Christmas," embossed holly, 3-1/4" l . . $2

Card Order Board

Elmira Greeting Card Co., blue fold-out display unit,
  Santa on sleigh on cover, 1958, 13" h. $7

*Cast iron candleholders, green with red berry trim, mkd.
"PAT'D 5-17-21," USA, 5" l, $12 each*

Candy Box

Boot shaped box, contained 10 pops & twirl-a-way
  game & a plastic boot, E. Rosen Co., Providence,
  RI, 5-1/2" h $10
"Charms," 5 lb. box, paper label, winter scene,
  7-1/2"x10"x3". $10
"Christmas Greetings," Three Wise Men on camels,
  "assorted chocolates," Wayne Candies, Fort
  Wayne, IN, 7-1/2"x11"x3" $15
"Merry Christmas," cloth handle, Candy Corp. Amer-
  ica, three toy soldiers pictured, 1934,
  3"x 4-1/2"x1-3/4" $6
"Merry Christmas," pictured—chalet winter scene
  framed by holly, 7-1/2" hx10" l x 3" deep. . . . $10
"Merry Christmas," 5 lb. box, "chocolate coated Christ-
  mas candy," winter scene, 1920s, 7-1/2"x11"x3" $9
"Merry Christmas, Happy New Year," string handle,
  Santa face in a wreath, 1920s, 3 x 4-1/2"x1-3/4" $5
Santa face, string handle, USA, 1970s, 3"x4-1/2"x
  1-3/4". $3
Schoolhouse shaped red box, Candle Novelty Co., A
  Coppers Product, Kearny, NJ, 4" h $10
Snowman-shaped front, green box with white snow-
  man, 6-1/2" h. $20
Three carolers with Tudor style street background,
  USA, 1930, 3"x4-1/2"x1-3/4" $5
Triangle-shaped box, string handle, Santa, sleigh
  and deer in silhouette over snow covered village,
  mkd. "Made in USA," 8" l $35
Two reindeer in trees, cloth handle, James P. Linette
  Co., Womelsdorf, PA, 1990s, 3"x4-1/2"x1-3/4" $2

Dollar Bill

Real dollar bill with George Washington's picture covered with a Santa Claus, Riverside Market Christmas promotion for the Salvation Army, 1991 . . .$3

Gift Tag

"A Merry Yuletide," children caroling, mkd. "USA,"
  2-3/4" l. $2
"Christmas Greetings," scene of Bethlehem, mkd.
  "Made in USA," 2-3/4" l $2
"Merry Christmas," embossed poinsettias, 3" l . . $2
"Merry Christmas," folded card, scene thru a church
  window, printed in Germany, 2-1/4" h $4

*Lantern, 4-sided with peaked top with wire bail, metal candle-
holder in base, black cardboard and colored tissue paper
Christmas scenes, 1940s, USA, 9-1/2" h, $25*

Metal candle clips, lacquered colors $3 ea. except Santa $12

Greeting Card

"A Hearty Christmas Greeting," children playing in snow, paper lace trim, 1900, 4" l $5

"At Christmas," ornaments on tree, "Scent O'Pine," USA, 1950s, 6" h $3

"Best Christmas Wishes," winter scene, card held together with ribbon, Germany, 1932, 4-1/2" h . . $6

Christmas bonus announcement, decorated with poinsettia and holly, 1916, 6" l $7

"Christmas Greetings," Santa on the cover, story inside, held together with cloth ribbon, Art Lithograph Pub. Co., 1925, 6-1/2" h $10

"Christmas Greetings In My House," pop-up card, house with cat on the fence, 1925, 5" h $6

"Merry Christmas," girl decorating tree, "A Sunshine Card," mkd. "Made in USA," 1960, 4" h $4

Set of six envelopes each fitting in the next, each envelope decorated, Santa on the card in the smallest envelope, American Greeting Publisher, Cleveland, USA, 1933 . . . . $10

"Wishing You A Happy Christmas," two birds pictured on branch, sepia tones, Raphael Tuck & Sons, London, Saxony, 1900, 3" h $12

World War II card, Santa sitting on top of US plane circling over Europe, " la Photolith," I. Delaporte, Paris, 6-1/2" h $8

Menu

Christmas dinner, Company A, 66th Infantry and Headquarters Company 66th Infantry, Fort George G. Meade, MD, 1935, 6" h $10

Postcard

"A Merry Christmas," an African American man delivering a turkey to an African American woman standing in the doorway of her log cabin, c. 1906 by I.P.C.N. Co. $10

"A Merry Christmas To You," Santa writing, basket of toys at his feet, sitting in woods, talking to angel, printed in Germany, series 9593, 1909 . . . . . $8

"Best Wishes For A Merry Christmas," plum pudding sitting on sled, signed Ellen H. Clapsaddle, Inter-national Art Pub. Co., No. 51340, New York, printed in Germany $7

"Loving Christmas Wishes," embossed printing, Father Christmas and holly, over printed in gold, Germany, 1905 . . . . $5

"Joyeux Noel," photo card, girl putting doll in carriage with Christmas tree in background, WWI soldier's card $4

Santa in sleigh with two deer, pastel colors, embossed with gold highlights, 1908 . . . . $7

Program

Christmas service, St. John's Rectory, South Williamsport, PA, 1925 . . . . $3

Seals

Cellophane package, "Christmas Greetings" on package Santa Claus seals, USA, pkg. 3-3/4" h $5

Glassine envelope with Santa titled "Special 10 cent assortment, USA," variety of holiday seals inside, envelope 3" l $5

Glassine envelope, wreath seals, mkd. "Made in Saxony," 2-1/2" h $10

Stereograph card

One side pictures Santa peeking in through the keyhole, the second side pictures children peeking out the keyhole at Santa, Keystone View Co., Meadville, PA and St. Louis, Mo., 1899, 6-1/2" l $15

Two light candolier with brush Christmas tree and Mazda lamps, original box mkd. "#46 Littwin Electric Manuf. Corp., NYC," 15" h $40

PUTZ

Animals, Birds, Etc.

Celluloid

Alligator, cream, USA, 3" l $8
Antelope, red, mkd. "Occupied Japan," 3-1/4" h $12
Bear
    black, mkd. "Japan," 2-1/4" h $12
    polar, mkd. "Japan," 2" h $10
    polar, white
2-1/4" lx1-1/4" h $6
    3-1/2" lx2-1/2" h $10
    10" lx5-1/2" h $75
Buffalo, black and brown, mkd. "Irwin," 2" h . . . $15
Chick, yellow, 3/4" h $6
Dog, brown, collar, mkd. "Japan," 2" h $7
Duck, green and white, 1" h $6
Fish, brown, 1-1/2" l $5
Frog, green and yellow, 1-1/2" l $7
Giraffe, yellow with brown spots, mkd. "Occupied Ja-
    pan," 4" h $15
Goose, gray and white, 2" h $6
Hippopotamus
    gray, mkd. "Tokyo Japan," 2" h $10
    purple, mkd. "Occupied Japan," 2-1/2" h $15

German composition Nativity figures, Three Wise Men $20 ea.

Leopard, red with black spots, 1-1/2" h $7
Lion, brown, 2-1/2" h $8
Ostrich, brown, blue and white, mkd. "Occupied Ja-
    pan," 3-1/2" h $15
Parrot in cage, cage red & black, 1-1/2" h $15
Pheasant, metal legs, pink and brown, 1-1/2" h . $6
Pig, pink, mkd. "USA," 1-1/4" h $6
Rhino, gray, mkd. "USA," 2" h $12
Seal, brown, mkd. "Made in Japan," 2-1/4" l $6
Stork, red and white, 3" h $8
Swan, gray and white, mkd. "USA," 1" h $5
    1-1/2" h $8
Tiger, beige and black, mkd. "USA," 2-1/4" h . . $10
Turkey, gobbler, metal legs, blue, 2" h $10
Turkey, hen, metal legs, brown and black, 1-1/2" h$8
Turtle, brown, 2-1/4" l $5
Zebra, white with black stripes, mkd. "Occupied Ja-
    pan," 2" h $8

Animals, Birds, Etc.

Composition, Germany

Cat, sitting, 1-1/2" h $18
Chick, metal feet, 1" h $10
Dog, sitting, 1" h $18
Dog, wooden legs, standing1-1/2" h $20
Duck, metal feet, 1-1/2" h $10
Flamingo, metal feet, 2-1/2" h $15
Giraffe, yellow with brown spots, wooden legs and
    horns, cloth ears and tail, 5-1/2" h $55
Goose, metal feet, 1-3/4" h $12
Hen, metal feet, 2" h $12

Candle, electrified, red cardboard with green base trimmed with foil holly, 9-1/2" h $15

Nativity scene, cardboard fold-out, 1950s, Sweden, 7" h, $8

Jackal, gray and black, wooden legs, 2" h. $40
Leopard, hide covered, yellow and black, glass
    eyes, 3" h. $45
Lion, yellow, string tail, 2-1/2" h. $35
Rooster, metal feet, 2" h $12
Peacock, metal feet, tail closed, feather crest, 2" h $15
Pelican, metal feet, 2" h. $15
Pheasant, metal feet, tail down, 2" h. $12
Pheasant, metal feet, tail up, 3" h $12
Pig, pink, 1-1/2" h $30
Pigeon, metal feet, 1" h. $15
Seagull, metal feet, 1" h. $15
Skunk, black and white, 1-1/2" h. $15
Songbird, metal feet, 3/4" h. $10
Stork, metal feet, 2" h $15
Swan, painted feet, 1-1/2" h $15
Swan, covered with white rabbit fur, paper label,
    2-1/2" h $35
Turkey, metal feet, hen, 1" h $15
Turkey, gobbler, metal feet, tail fanned, 2-1/2" h $20
Zebra, hide covered, black and white, glass eyes,
    wooden legs, 3" h $45

Animals, Glass

Penguin, blown, black and white, 2" h. $20
Penguin, blown, silver and white, Germany, 7" h. .$60

Animals, Plastic

Cow, gray, 1960s, 2-1/4" h $3
Horse, black, 1960s, 2-1/4" h $3
Pig, white, 1960s, 1" h. $3

Animals, Rubber

Chicken, beige, molded, 1-1/4" h. $6
Cow, black and beige, 2" h $8
Horse, brown, 4" h. $10

Buildings

Church, paper, dresden rose window, white mica
    with gold trim, cellophane windows, mkd. "Japan,"
    7" wx10-1/2" h $65

European church with music box, wood, white,
    green and brown, 6-1/2" lx6" h $35
House, cardboard, bright colors, sponge trees at-
    tached to base, mkd. "Japan," 3" wx2-1/2" h. $12
House, cardboard, detailed multicolored painting,
    mkd. "Germany," 3" h $7
House, cardboard, European architecture, litho-
    graph, 1-1/2"x2" h $10
House, cardboard, heavily trimmed in "snow,"
    sponge trees, printed tissue windows, mkd. "Ja-
    pan," 5" wx4" h $15
Fences
    cast iron, silver with gold trim, individual posts, fif-
        teen 12" sections $150
    plastic, white picket, "Plasticville," six sections,
        2" h. $20
    wood, dyed red, nine 6" folding sections, 3" h $45
    wood, brown posts, wired for lighting on end
        posts, homemade, six 2' l sections $60

Miscellaneous

Spun glass angel hair, original box, Santa carrying
    pack on front of box, "leMarc Novelty Co., New
    York 3, NY," box 8" h. $7

Nuremberg or Erzgebrige Penny Woodens

Animals
    cow, brown and white, 3/4" h. $10
    dog, yellow with red collar, 1/2" h $10
Carts/Cars
    horse drawn wagon, green wagon, 2 gray horses,
        carrying 3 passengers, 2-3/4" l $30
    flats carriage pulled by team of white horses, driv-
        er, bride and groom, West Germany, 6" l . . $35
    log truck, blue with black metal wheels, driver,
        2-1/2" l $30
    sleigh and team of gray horses, two male figures
        riding in the sleigh, West Germany, 5-1/2" l $35
People
    couple sitting on park bench, pot metal, USA,
        2" h. $20
    elves, various poses, set of six, Germany, 1" h $65
    snowman band, Germany, 1-1/4" h. $80
    skater, pot metal, 2" h, USA $12

*Nativity set, hand-carved and hand-painted, 8 pieces, original
box mkd. "Made by the Peasants of the Tyrolean Alps," $30*

Sled rider, lying down on sled, pot metal, USA, 1-1/4" h $15

skier, two poles, pot metal, USA, 2" h $12

Trees, brush

3-1/2" h, green, mica snow, red wooden base. $4

4" h, green, mica snow, red wooden base. . . . $5

4-1/2" h, red, green tub base $6

6" h, green, mica snow, red wooden base. . . . $8

7" h, red, red wooden base $10

9" h, white, red wooden base. $12

9-1/2" h, white, red wooden base $13

10" h, green, red tub base, glass bead decorations, mica snow $15

13" h, green, mica snow red wooden base, very narrow $20

Trees, plastic

pine, hard plastic, green with brown base, mkd.(BB), 4" h $4

REINDEER

Celluloid

Beige, "elk type," mkd. "Made in USA," 2" h $6

Brown, "Made in USA," 3" h. $7

Brown with black spots, 3-1/2" h $7

Brown with white spots, paper label – "made in Japan," 4" h $8

Red and white, 3" h $8

White, 1 -1/4" h $5

White, painted eyes, 3" h. $8

White, painted eyes, pulling red and white sled, 3" h. $15

White with silver mica, red glass eyes, mkd. "Japan," 6"x6" h $30

White with silver mica, red glass eyes, mkd. "Japan" 4-1/2" h $15

Glass, Blown

Blue with brown antlers, standing, Germany, 4-1/4" h $35

"Christmas Manger Set #743," Concordia Product, USA, $20

Sheep, composition with flannel covering, wooden legs, mkd. Germany, 3-1/2" h $40

Pair, connected, silver, one standing and one lying down, Germany, 6-1/4" h $60

Silver, lying down, Germany, 2" h $20

White, standing, Germany, 3-1/4" h $20

Metal

Brown, lying down, mkd. "Germany," 3-1/2" h x 4-1/2" l $45

Brown, standing, mkd. "Germany," 6-1/2" hx8-1/2" l $75

Brown, standing, mkd. "Germany," 5-1/2" hx4" l $45

Brown, standing, mkd. "Germany," 2-1/2" hx2" l $25

Plastic

White, 1-1/2" h. $3

White, mkd. "USA," 3" h $4

Wax

Brown with white spots, cardboard base mkd. "Gurley Novelty Co., Buffalo, NY, copyright 1950, 3" h. . .$3

SANTA CLAUS FIGURES

Banks

Hard plastic Egg-shaped, "Firestone Bank," Lisbon, Ohio, 3" h. $7

Wearing a hat, "Knox Hats, NY," made in USA, original box, 6" h $25

Plaster

Santa sleeping in green stuffed chair, 1950s, 8" h $35

Donkey, brown, flocked, mkd. Germany, 3-1/2" h $35

Containers

Cardboard
Red, flocked, separates in middle, composition face, rabbit fur beard, mkd. "West Germany," 12-1/2" h $65

Hard Plastic
PEZ candy container, made in Austria, 3-3/4" h. $7
"Santa's Candy Express," red Santa, white sleigh and eight white reindeer, original box 15" l, produced by E. Rosen Co., Providence, RI, distributed by Sears, Roebuck and Co. Stores, original box contained "sweet candy pops" $40

Glass
Candy, metal screw-top base, clear with green long robe and hood, 5-1/2" h $120
Candy, metal screw-top base, clear with white long robe and hood, mkd. "AVOR. 1 oz., V.C., USA," 4-1/2" h $110
Candy, metal screw-top base, clear with red, yellow and black, climbing in chimney, "Victory Candy Co.," 5-1/2" h $140
Jelly jar, Kraft, metal top, 6-1/2" h $8
Perfume bottle, Avon, original box, "Here's My Heart Cologne," 3-1/2" h $10
Miscellaneous candy container, red net body, celluloid face, composition boots, Japan, 6-1/2" l . $85

Figures

Bisque
Running, red suit, mkd. "Japan," 1-3/4" h $20

Standing, red suit, Japan, 3" h $30
Standing, red suit, long coat, mkd. "Japan," 3-1/4" h $40
Standing, red suit, short coat, mkd. "Japan," 4" h . $40
Standing, red suit, mkd. "USA," 1-1/2" h $20

Cardboard
Making toys, with hobby horse in pack, easel back, 12" h $15
Sitting in white sleigh with mica, red suit, 4" l . . $10
Standing, easel back, 1940, 10" h $15
Standing and waving, multicolored, 3-1/2" h $8

Celluloid
Multicolored, in car, 4" l $65
Red, standing, arms at side, Irwin, USA, 1-1/4" h $20
Red, standing on brown metal skis, celluloid ski poles, Irwin, USA, 4" h. $40
Red and white, one piece unit Santa, sleigh and deer, Japan, 3-1/2" l $25
Red and white, one piece unit Santa, sleigh and deer, USA, 3-1/2" l. $30
Red and white, one piece unit Santa, sleigh and deer, sleigh is a "shell-like" boat, Japan, 4" l. $40
Red suit and red pointed hat, forked beard, Irwin Co., USA, 4-1/4" h. $40
Red suit, in round chimney, Irwin Co., USA, 3-1/2" h $45
Red suit, in white sleigh pulled by deer, 2 pcs., Japan, 1-1/2" h $15
Red suit, standing and holding a tennis racket, Japan, 3" h $35
Red suit, standing on "Merry Christmas" block with green bag of toys, USA, 3-3/4" h. $60
Red suit, standing with arms full of toys, USA, 4" h $50
Red, white and black, standing and waving, Japan, 2-1/4" $25
Red, white and green, sitting in red sleigh holding whip, string and celluloid harness holds two white deer with red glass eyes, 16" l. $110
Red, white and green, standing in round chimney, 4" h $50
White with red and green, driving snow covered car, house and tree on back of car, USA, 4" l $75

Czechoslovakian church and house, wire hangers, 3" h $12 ea.

White with red and green, sleigh and deer, Irwin Co., USA, 7" l $65

White with red highlight, in car, 3" l $75

Chalk

Red suit, on blue skis, stamped "England" on base, 2-1/4" h $25

Red suit, rowing boat on water, stamped "England" on base, 1-1/2" h $25

Red suit, with boy on sled, stamped "England" on base, 1-1/2" h......................... $25

Red suit, with open toy bag at feet, stamped "England" on base, 2" h.................... $25

Red suit, with tree over shoulder, stamped "England" on base, 2-1/2" h $25

Composition

Red flannel coat and hat, blue flannel pants, composition face, hands and boots, wire body, rabbit fur beard, Germany, 7-1/2" h $125

Red flannel coat, blue cloth pants, cotton hands and beard, made in Japan, 6" h $80

Red flannel coat, blue pants, rabbit fur beard, stands on wooden base, red and green wicker basket on back, holding feather tree, mkd. "Germany" on base, 9" h............................ $400

Composition/Plaster Overlay

Father Christmas

Blue coat with gold flecks, black boots, Germany, 9-3/4" h $1000

Blue coat with silver mica, black boots, Germany, 8" h................................... $900

Green coat, black boots, Germany, 9-1/2" h . $1200

Red coat, black boots, Germany,
   8" h.................................. $500
   10-1/2" h $700
   14-1/4" h $850

Set of cardboard houses with celluloid figures, original box, Japan $60

Celluloid Santa Claus, wire hanger, Irwin Co., USA, 3-1/2" h $55

Yellow coat, black boots, Germany,
   6-1/4" h............................. $550
   7-1/4" h............................. $750
   9-3/4" h $850

White coat with silver mica, black boots, Germany,
   7" h $350
   9-1/2" h $600

White coat with silver mica, black boots, metal hanger on top, Germany, 6" h $300

Cotton Batting

Red body with chenille trim, black boots, composition face, holding foil holly leaf, 7" h $90

White body, black boots, composition face, 10" h $110

Egg Crate Pressed Cardboard

Red, large pack on back, climbing into chimney, 10" h..................................... $95

Red and black, hands in pockets, 10" h $90

Red, head tilted to one side, 10" h $90

Red with white, black and yellow, mkd. "S4 ATCO Co.," 9-1/2" h $80

White with red and yellow, in sleigh with deer on snow, 10-1/2" l........................ $65

White with red, pink and black, red net pack on back, "Harry and David, Medford, Oregon" paper label inside base, 9-1/2" h $85

Chromolithograph angels with tinsel trim, Germany, 8-1/2" h $20

Hard Plastic

Blue suit, standing, holding a tool, 3-1/2" h $15
Red suit, riding red bike with yellow wheels, 3-1/2" h$10
Red, rotund, hole for light in back, 15" h $20
Red suit, sitting in sleigh pulled by deer, all one
    piece, 4-1/2" l. $20
Red suit, standing in cart pulled by three white deer,
    blowing yellow horn, "Santa's Candy Wagon" in
    white on cart, 9" h $30
Red suit, standing in chimney and waving, 5" h $15
Red suit, standing on white snowshoes, 4-1/2" h. .$12
Red suit, standing, snow globe in belly, Hong Kong,
    6" h. $15
Red and white suit, flat with small stand, 4-1/2" h $8
Red, with small pack in right hand, hole for light in
    back, Union Product 811G, Leominster, Mass.,
    13-1/2" h $20
Red with white and black, standing, plastic bar be-
    tween feet, electrified, 17" h. $35

Miscellaneous

Mr. and Mrs. Claus, red flocked soft plastic bodies,
    Hong Kong, 7" h. $12
Pere Noel and Baby Jesus, hard cotton face, che-
    nille and tissue paper clothing and decorations,
    cotton beard on wood board, mkd. "Made in
    France," 4" h $55

Santa bell, cotton batting head and arms, papier-
    mâché "bell body," black composition boots at-
    tached to wires hanging out bottom of bell, 4" l$100
Santa driving sleigh red felt coat, composition face,
    composition deer, white frosted wood sleigh, Ja-
    pan, 8-1/2" l. $95
Santa driving sleigh, red felt coat, composition face,
    standing in a white and pink cardboard sleigh cov-
    ered with pink paper, two composition deer, Ja-
    pan, 6" l. $85
Santa face on cardboard boot, composition face,
    cotton beard, red flannel hat, Japan, 4-1/2" h $70
Santa in airplane, red cotton body, composition face,
    cardboard airplane with silver glitter, dist. by Mont-
    gomery Ward stores, 6-1/4" l. $65
Santa in airplane, red cotton body, composition face,
    red cardboard airplane with wooden wheels, Ja-
    pan, 5-1/2" l. $75
Santa in canoe, red cotton body with composition
    face, cardboard canoe with silver glitter, dist. by
    Montgomery Ward stores, 2" h $65
Santa in canoe, red with white and black cotton batting,
    pink celluloid canoe, Santa 2-1/2", canoe 5" l. . $70
Santa in sailboat, red cotton body with composition
    face, cardboard sailboat with silver glitter, dist. by
    Montgomery Ward stores, 4" h $65
Santa on skis, red coat, beige cloth pants and pack,
    wrapped straw body, composition face, cotton beard,
    fiberboard skis and wooden poles, Japan, 6" h. . $95
Santa riding bird, molded cardboard bird body cov-
    ered in white cotton, movable white feather wings,
    gold stick legs, Santa has cotton face, hung on
    spring, wings flapped when bounced up and
    down, Japan, 6" l. $65

*Chromolithograph green coated Father Christmas standing on
a crescent moon, tinsel trim, 1890s, Germany, 7" h $45*

Santa sitting on child's sled, red flannel coat, composition face, rabbit fur beard, Germany, 5" l . $185

Santa sitting on white cotton batting ball, cotton head and beard, tissue paper hat, pipe cleaner legs, mkd. "Made in France," 3-1/2" h $60

Santa standing, red chenille coat and body, composition face, cotton beard, Japan, 5-1/2" h . . . $60

Santa standing, red chenille pipe cleaner body, paper face, cotton beard, Japan, 5" h $20

Santa standing, red flannel coat, blue cotton pants, composition face and black boots, cotton beard, black oilcloth belt, holding brown stuffed sack over shoulder, white frosted cardboard base mkd. "Japan," 7-1/2" h $90

Santa standing, red flocked paper coat, black oilcloth belt, cotton batting hands, plastic face, cotton beard, holding plastic candle in one hand and white plastic bell in other hand, cardboard disk base, Japan, 5-3/4" h $45

Santa standing, red flocked paper coat, black oilcloth belt, cotton batting hands, pressed cardboard face, cotton beard, holding brush tree, cardboard disk base, Japan, 5" h $40

Santa standing next to turret-like building, cotton Santa, composition face, cardboard building, building 4" h $70

Santa standing, white chenille pipe cleaner body, composition face, cotton beard, 2-1/2" h $15

Cotton batting camel, brown, 3-1/2" h $55

Papier-mâché

Red, pack in front, 10-1/2" h $90

Red with gold, white and yellow, rotund with hand raised, 9" h $80

Red with white and yellow, standing, 4" h $55

Red with white and yellow, standing, 4-1/2" h . . $70

Red and white, black top hat, standing, 10" h . . $90

White with orange trim, large pack on back, 5" h $50

White with red and black, 4" h $45

White with red and green, in chimney, long beard, 9" h $125

White with red and green, in sleigh, 8"x6-1/2" h $80

White with red and yellow highlights, 3-1/2" h . . $40

White with red, yellow and green, pack on back, 7" h $65

White with red, black, and yellow, green pack to side, 9" h $75

Mask

Red cloth head, buckram face, cotton beard and eyebrows, 11" l $30

Lantern

Glass bulb is standing figure, metal "AMICO," metal base mkd. "Japan," 5-1/2" h $45

Plate

Child's plate, Santa's face painted on plate, USA, 4" h $30

Cotton batting pear, mica highlights, paper leaf, wire hanger, 1920-1930, Japan, 3" h $12

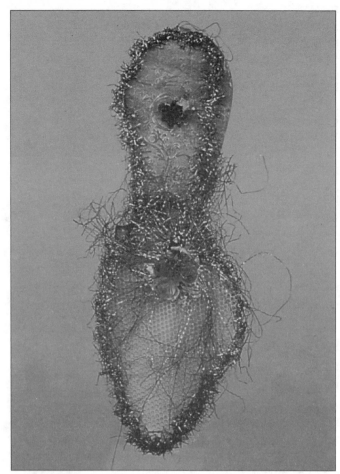

Dresden slipper, flat with net upper and tinsel trim, early 1900s, Germany, 7-1/2" h $45

Spoon

Silverplate, stocking on chimney and "Merry Christmas" on top side of handle, "Happy New Year" on back of handle, Santa and sleigh on bowl of spoon, 4" l $40

Store Display

Pressed cardboard, flat back, Santa head, glitter highlights, 18" h $75

Toys

Battery Operated

Doll, cloth-stuffed body and head, composition boots, Buckram face with painted features, red cloth suit and hat, human hair beard, 17" h . $160

Composition body, moveable arms legs and head, red flannel suit and pack, black oil cloth belt, 18" h. $250

Rubber, holding pack and bell, "Ashland Rubber Products Corp.," "Toytime," 10" h $40

Rubber, waving, "SC" on belt, "Rempel Manufacturing Inc.," Akron, Ohio, 11" h $45

Rubber, with squeaker inside, 6-1/2" h $25

Stuffed, "Hallmark Co.," 7" h $15

Stuffed body, red plush suit, black felt mittens and boots, hard plastic face, 22" h $40

Pop-up hard plastic chimney-shaped box with pop-up soft plastic Santa head, red and white, 4" h . . .$14

Pull toy in sleigh soft plastic, wheels in base, mkd. "made in Japan," 3-1/2" h $20

Standing, holding candy cane, red suit, hard plastic, 5" h $12

Standing on four wheels, hard plastic, "Fun World Inc.," New York, NY, mkd. "made in Hong Kong," 3-3/4" h $15

Roly poly pressed cardboard, Santa has clown-like features, 7" h $450

Red plush body, soft plastic face, musical, cloth label mkd. "A Gunderful Creation, made in Japan," 9" h$20

Red suit, bell inside, Kiddie Prod. Inc., Avon, Mass., 4" h $8

Metal base, metal packages, plastic face, cloth body, Santa draws packages out of pack while ringing bell, 9" h $95

Metal, ringing bell, mkd. "made in Japan," holding sign "Merry Christmas," 6" h $70

Metal body and base, plastic face, cloth pack, bell and turns head, 9-1/2" h $85

Metal body and base, reads book and turns pages with magnet on hand, Japan, 7-1/2" h. $80

Riding bike, celluloid figure, metal bike, mkd. "made in Japan," 3-1/2" h $55

Riding reindeer, plastic head, Japan, 6" h $50

Rubber, jumps in place, 5" h $55

Seated on chimney ringing bell, plastic head and face, lithograph base and chimney, mkd. "made in Japan," 10" h $90

Tin house and chimney, plastic face, ring bell while sitting on house top, 9-1/2' h $85

Walker doll, pull string in belly, cloth coat, paper label mkd. "Germany," 6-1/2" h $45

Wind-up driving green metal sleigh with wheels and bell, red celluloid Santa, white celluloid deer, wheel causes deer to move, mkd. "Made in Occupied Japan," original box, 8-1/2" l $95

Dresden swan, flat, gold with silver, green and red highlights, early 1900s, Germany, 5"x6" $90

SNOWMEN
Cardboard
Flat, chenille arms, holding tree, black & white,
3-3/4" h $5
With silver mica, cotton head, Japan, 3" h. . . $10
Chalk
Candleholder, red, black & white, 7" h. $12
Cotton
Foil hat, chenille & paper trim, Occupied Japan,
6" h. $20
Glass
Head and body, painted features, foil pointed hat,
chenille trim, Japan 4" h. $7
Perfume bottle, Avon, paper label, "hat" screw-top
lid, 3-1/2" h. $6
Snow globe, plastic base, holding blue balloon, Aus-
tria, 5" h $25

Hard Plastic
Holding black & white lantern, lighted, original box,
"Paramount Illuminated Snowman #62," manufac-
tured by Raylite Elec. Corp., New York, NY,
6-1/2" h $22
Holding hat, black & white, 3" h. $7
PEZ candy container, made in Yugoslavia, 4-3/4" h $5
Salt & pepper shakers, Mr. & Mrs. on red hard plastic
ribbon tray, J.S., New York, Hong Kong, 3-1/2" h $7

Molded Cardboard
Open base, red hat and scarf, orange nose holding stick,
mkd. "Germany," candy container, 5-1/2" h $95
Red and white with silver mica, hard plastic red hat,
3-1/4" h $6
Papier-mâché
White, red net sack, paper label on opening in bot-
tom mkd. "Harry and David," 10" h $70

Wood
Smoker, Germany, 6" h. $45

Dresden 3 dimensional bulldog, early 1900s, mkd. Germany, 3" h $250

Glass balls with paper caps, L-R, blue, 3-1/2" h $15, clear with lacquer stripes, 2-1/3" h $8

TREES/WREATHS
Aluminum
Tree, metal pole, metal stand, 4' h $40
Brush
Wreath, green with white mica trim, multicolored
glass beads, red cloth ribbon, wire hanger, Japan,
3" d $4
Green with white mica trim, red and gold ribbon,
6" d $15
Red with white mica trim, wire hanger, Japan, 4" d $6
Cellophane
Tree, green, white wooden base, 3' h $25
Wreath, red, electrified red and silver cardboard candle
attached to base, chenille poinsettia trim, 7" d . $15
Chenille
Wreath, red with green erikamoos and white frosted
cloth poinsettias, 7" h $8
Egg Crate
Pressed cardboard tree, green with red and yellow
base, 11" h $75
Feather Tree
Green, red wood tub, Germany, 1" h. $12
Green, white wooden base with stenciled holiday de-
sign, Germany, 3' h $300
Green with red composition berries on end of
branches, candleholders on branches, white
round wooden base, Germany, 6' h $600
White with red composition berries, red wood round
base, West Germany, 12" h $75
Visca
Tree, green, white wooden round base, USA, 12" h $25
Tree, white, white wooden square base, USA, 4' h $60

Glass figural songbird on metal clip with spring legs, spun glass tail, 1920-1930, Germany, 5" l $15

Glass beaded ornament, Japan, 8" h $20

Glass figural, house, Germany, 3" h $35

Glass figural, Santa, Germany, 2-1/2" h $25

China red and white Santa with blue pack, Japan, 1-3/4" $15, china girl Christmas shopping, Japan, 2" h $12

Red and white plastic lion, plastic hook, 3-1/2" h $5

Papier-mâché tree ornaments, male figures, 5-1/2" h, Germany, each $45

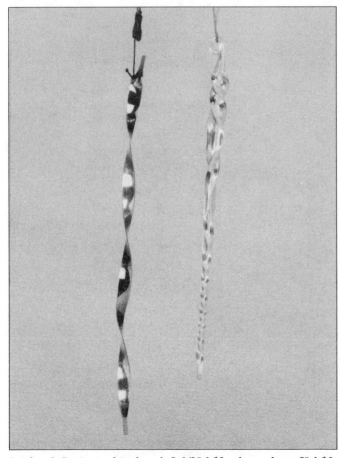

Icicles, L-R, tin, multicolored, 5-1/2" l $2, glass, clear, 5" l $3

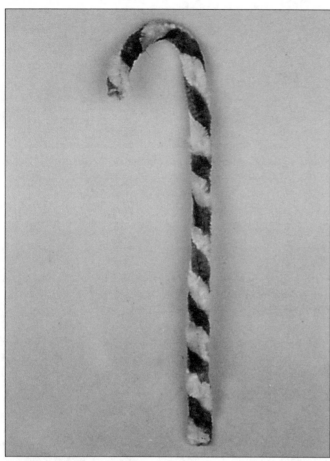

Chenille candy cane, 6" h, 1930s $5

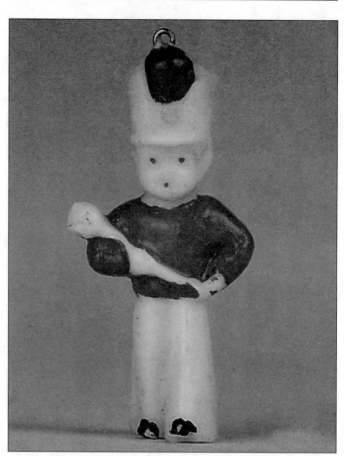

Wax hollow drummer boy with metal ring in hat, 3" h, USA $5

Christmas cards, "Christmas Greetings," The Art Lithographic Pub. Co., printed in Munich, Germany, 1884, 6" h $15, "Christmas Greetings In My House," USA, 1920s, 5" h $8

Candy boxes, L-R, "Merry Christmas" Santa with sleigh, 5-1/2" h $8, "Merry Christmas," mkd. Printed in USA, "handbag style," 6-1/2" h $12, "Merry Christmas," Santa in workshop, 5-1/2" l $10

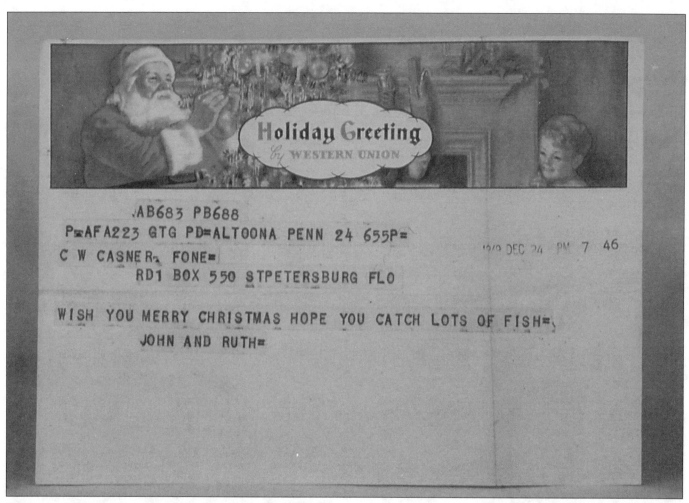

Telegram, "Holiday Greeting by Western Union," 1946 $10

Postcards, L-R, Germany, $10 ea.

L-R, hard plastic green tree with brown base, mkd. "BB," 4" h $3, brush tree, green with white mica, red wooden base, 4-3/4" h $7

Christmas card holder, Gibson Card Co., Cincinnati, OH, 26-1/2" lx8" h $35

Celluloid animals, L-R, beige elephant $10, deer $7, swan $6

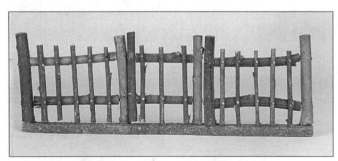

One section of twig fence, Germany, 9" l $12

Celluloid, (L) Santa in chimney, Irwin Co., USA, 4" h, $40 (R) Santa driving a car, Irwin Co., USA, 4" l $50

Santa bank, rubber, mkd. "Christmas Club A Corp., NY, 1972," 6" h $25

Hard plastic Santa bank, mkd. "Fanny Farmer," 7" h $35

Composition chicken, with beading, metal legs, Germany, 1-1/2" h $12

Log houses, mkd. "Germany," L-R, A Frame cottage $20, cabin $15

L-R, "Spun Glass Angel's Hair" $7, "Christmas Snow" $5

Red flocked cardboard Santa, container separates at belly, mkd. "West Germany" inside, 6" h $35

Gift boxes, holly berries & leaves, USA, 7" x 3", $8 and poinsettia & holly, USA, 5 -1/2" x 4", $5

"Flats," Germany, skaters set $40

"Flats," Germany, elf $12; Santa $60; snowman bandleader $15

Built-rite buildings, USA, house, 5" h $18, fire station, 5" h $20

Cardboard Santa with easel back, 1950s, USA, 12" h $6

Composition Santa with red flannel coat and hood, West Germany, 11" h $85

Metal sled rider, mkd. "Made in France," 2-1/4" h $28

Santa bank, metal, marked, "Save Time and Money, Bank of West Virginia," dist. 1968-1969, 5-1/2" h, $55

Santa and train candy container, Santa face is composition with cotton beard, train's is cardboard with mica coating, label mkd. "Japan," 6" l $85

Metal deer, mkd. "Germany," 5" h $45

"Flats," Germany, skiing set $42

Celluloid Santa, sleigh and three brown caribou, mkd. "Japan," 22" l $90

Candy container, composition Santa with red flannel coat and hood with mica, log base, mkd. "Germany," 4" h $250

Santa Claus candy container, glass, plastic screw-top head, USA, 5-1/2" h $55

Santa Claus candy container, glass, screw-top base, 8" h $500

Chalk Santa, mkd. "England," 2-1/4" h $15

Cardboard Santa, mkd. on back, "1st National Bank of Blooms-burg, Bloomsburg, PA," 7" h $10

Pennsylvania chalk Father Christmas figures, blue with gold pack, solid, 5-1/2" h, $1400 and black/brown with smears of mica and snow, hollow mold, 7" h, $2000

Hard plastic, USA, L-R, riding a deer, 9" h $18; with toy bag, 7-1/2" h $15

A group of American-made pressed cardboard Santas, standing Santas 10" h, each $95, Santa and sleigh, 10" l, $70

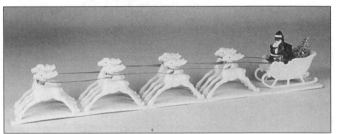

Hard plastic, Santa, sleigh and eight reindeer, 20-1/2" l $30

Hard plastic Santa, 5" h $12

Hard plastic Santa on green skis, mkd. "Rosbro Products," USA, 4-1/2" h $15

Santa trio, soft plastic with flocked coating, L-R, 6" h $4; turns on chimney base to "Jingle Bells," 14" h $20; 8" h $6

Santa Claus, sleigh and reindeer, composition Santa with flannel coat and pants, rabbit fur beard, composition deer and wooden sleigh, Germany, 18" h, 1910, $525

Composition Santa and moss goat cart, Germany, 9" l $200

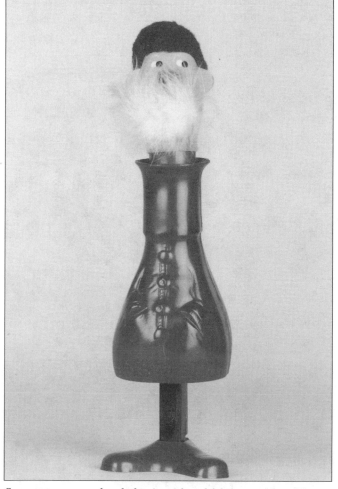

Santa pop-up toy, hard plastic with red felt hat, sold as "Santa Pops, Automatic Jack-In-The-Box," Tigrett Industries, USA, 1956, 9-1/2" h $30

Wind-up toy, celluloid Santa and deer, green metal sleigh, 1930s, Japan, 8-1/2" h, $65

Composition Santa, paper label on base - "Schoenhut Roly Poly, Patented Dec. 18, 1908," USA, 9-1/2" h, $800

Santa pop-up toy, cardboard chimney box, composition face and cloth coat, 1920s, Germany, 5-1/2" h, $130

Wind-up Santa, rings bell and waves celluloid balloons, 1930s, Japan, 7" h, $60

Santa "Wilson Walkies," fiberboard cone body with chenille trim, tissue paper hat, mkd. "Made in USA," original box, 5" h, $60

Wind-up rubber Santa, jumps in place, 5" h $50

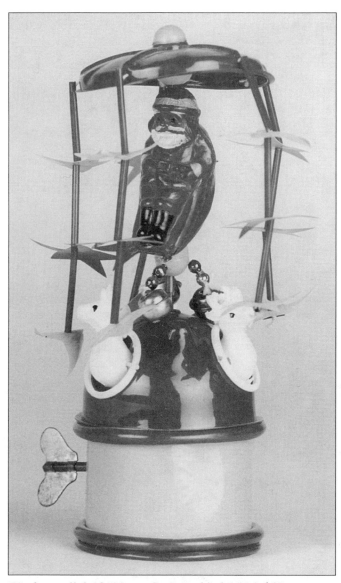

Wind-up celluloid "Merry-Go-Round," 6-1/2" h $65

Hard plastic snowman, 9-3/4" h $20

Hard plastic snowman, carrying red broom and yellow snow shovel, mkd. "Rosbro Plastics, Prov., RI," 5" h $12

Molded cardboard snowman, mkd. "Kentucky Tavern," 12 -1/4" h $85

BIBLIOGRAPHY

Agel, Jerome and Shulman, Jason. *The Thanksgiving Book*. New York: Dell Pub., 1987.

Dupuy, Trevor, Nevitt, ed. *Holidays*. New York: Franklin Watts Inc., 1965.

Gray, Nada. *Holidays – Victorian Women Celebrate in Pennsylvania*. Lewisburg, PA: Oral Traditions *Project of The Union County Historical Society*, 1983.

Ickis, Marguerite. *The Book Of Festival Holidays*. New York: Dodd, Mead & Co., 1964.

Lee, Ruth, Webb. *A History of Valentines*. New York: The Studio Publications Inc., 1952

Shoemaker, Alfred, L. *Christmas In Pennsylvania*. Kutztown, PA: Pennsylvania Folklife Society, 1959.

Smith, Dick and Smith, Lissa. *Christmas Collectibles*. Secaucus, NJ: Chartwell Books, 1993.

Snyder, Phillip, V. *December 25th*. New York: Dodd, Mead & Co., Inc., 1985.

Snyder, Phillip, V. *The Christmas Tree Book*. New York: Penguin Books, 1976.

Watts, Alan, W. *Easter*. New York: Henry Schuman, 1950.

AFTERWORD

Our last piece of advice is perhaps the most important–how to store your holiday treasures. If you are like many collectors you will leave your collection out all year long. However, some people only display their collections during the appropriate holidays. Regardless of how and when you decide to display your antiques you will need to follow a few basic guidelines.

When you bring home your "finds" dust them lightly with a very soft brush. A small paintbrush or a make-up "blush" brush can whisk away dirt without taking away paint. Water is the number one enemy of holiday decorations. Many items have been ruined over the years from water seeping into attics and basements. Consequently, use water sparingly to clean only plastic and celluloid. Your best bet is to consider the condition when purchasing—if the object is filthy and does not have a surface that is easily cleaned—think twice before purchasing it for your collection.

If you do choose to store your collection between holidays select a room where you can control the heat and humidity. Fluctuations in temperature can cause materials to crack or craze. Moisture dissolves lacquers and paints and promotes the growth of mildew. The temperature fluctuations of attics and the humidity of basements have destroyed family decorations.

The final storage tips are about wrapping. Tissue paper has been the time honored "wrap" for Christmas and other holiday decorations. Unfortunately it is also very abrasive and can damage the surface of a glass ornament or a painted object. Our suggestion is to wrap your collection in soft cotton cloth. Old sheets or pillowcases work great for storage. We often "nest" fragile items in divided boxes padded with cotton. It is also important to remove old hooks or wires from glass Christmas ornaments before storage. They often poke holes in the glass or craze paint surfaces.

Like all collectors—holiday collectors are dedicated and proud of their compilation. Holiday decorations bring very special smiles to people's faces so be sure to share your display with family, friends, co-workers, anyone—the smiles make it all worthwhile. Good luck in the continuous pursuit of holiday antiques and collectibles!